CW00956453

CONTEMPORARY ISSUES ON NATIONAL DEVELOPMENT

Essays on the Roles of Philosophy and
Entrepreneurship on National Development
(FESTSCHRIPT OF DR. BASSEY UBONG)

Professor J. D Okoh

Cover design by: Art Painter
Library of Congress Control Number: 2018675309
Printed in the United States of America

DEDICATION

This book is dedicated to the Almighty God

FOREWORD

The question as to why some countries of the 'South' continue to be poor and thus derogatorily tagged 'underdeveloped' or the more benign 'developing' despite abundant natural and human resources that they have and the fact that they do not have to re-invent the wheel will continue to be asked. The puzzle has been on for decades, spurning several development theories by economists across the world.

Development theories ranged from the beginnings of economics as an academic discipline such as the pioneering work of Adam Smith in his analysis of capitalism in 1776 to Karl Marx's communist theory of 1933. Classical theories came after, as in the linear stages of growth models of Roy F. Harrod (1939), Evsey Domar (1946) and W. W. W. Rostow (1960) followed by structural change models including those of W. Arthur Lewis (1954) and Hollis Chenery (1960). The theory put forward by Robert Solow (1956) and Trevor Swan (1956) is classified as neo-classical.

International dependency models continued the search for explanation of the development of nations, succeeded by neo-classical counter-revolution models and contemporary theories such as coordination failure being the cause of underdevelopment. The coast is very wide and continues expanding with exciting ones such as the famous Paul Rosestein-Rodan's big push theory of 1943 and controversial ones such as immiserizing growth by Jagdish Bahgwati, as well as balanced or unbalanced growth and Amartya Sen's expansion of the concept of development beyond the material, to capabilities and freedoms. The horizon will continue to expand with time.

These theories have been discussed, tried, and apparently abandoned. More continue to be discussed and tried, yet, poor countries remain poor with vital economic indices crawling while developed countries continue to gallop far ahead. Apparently because conventional wisdom or words of elders hold that the axe must not rest until the difficult oak tree has been felled, more theories and effort will continue to be spurned. Nonetheless, the emerging economies such as China, India, Indonesia, Brazil appear to give some hope for the future. And we must mention the great leap of Singapore from underdevelopment to being one of the Newly Industrialized Countries (NICs) of the world today.

This is the rationale for this volume which looks at development from two perspectives that are focused: entrepreneurship as a precursor of development and as driven by educational institutions; and some philosophical issues that affect the trend and pace of national development. No one can doubt the fact that for any meaningful and sustained socio-economic development to take place, education must be at the fore-front. Education does not only prepare individuals for self-reliance and a better life, it is the basis of the forward movement of societies morally, politically, and socially.

In this volume, essays on diverse topics on theory and practice are presented, all aimed at highlighting the issue of societal development. The volume, a festschrift, is in two parts – entrepreneurship theory and practice and philosophy and national development. The festschrift is in honour of an academic, Dr. Bassey Ubong, former Provost/Chief Executive Officer of the Federal College of Education (Technical), Omoku, in Rivers State, Nigeria. The two aspects reflect the honouree's two areas of academic interest in the past eighteen years. The collection is introduced by the incumbent Chairman of the Governing Council of the College, Professor Aminu Mikailu. Professor Mikailu is an economist and a Management expert, has served twice as Vice Chancellor, and is currently teaching at Usmanu Danfodiyo University, Sokoto (former University of Sokoto) where he was once the Chief Executive. His contribution says something about the tenure of the honouree; it goes further to make a case for peace and national integration in Nigeria as a basis for national development. evidently based on his experience at Omoku where the College he is superintending over is located.

Dr. Bassey Ubong holds the Master's in business administration degree and has taught entrepreneurship for more than fifteen years in the College. He presented the first edition of the Inaugural Lecture of the College in 2013 when he was the Deputy Provost of the College. The Lecture was fittingly titled National development: Can entrepreneurship be the beautiful bride? The Lecture detailed his long foray into the practice, and later the theory of business. The first section of this festschrift opens with a practical paper by the 7th Vice Chancellor of the University of Port Harcourt, Rivers State, Nigeria, Professor J. A. Ajienka, whose tenure was devoted to making the institution an entrepreneurial university. This orientation should remind us of the role that academic institutions play in private sector development in advanced economies – the technopole concept.

The honouree also holds the Master and Doctor of Philosophy degrees in Philosophy of Education. Therefore, the second section of the book deals with issues related to values, educational philosophy, and policy as they affect national development. The section includes a paper by Professor A. M. Wokocha, former Provost of two Colleges of Education and former Registrar of the Teachers Registration Council of Nigeria. If education is to play the role it is expected in the development effort, then it should be an organized profession rather than being an activity for all comers. And a former Deputy Vice Chancellor of University of Port Harcourt, Professor J. D. Okoh who supervised Dr. Ubong's dissertation while in the PhD programme makes a strong contribution on moral philosophy.

The key feature of this collection of excellent papers from distinguished Professors and academics from universities and College of Education system is the emphasis on practicum. It is good to theorize, that being the primary engagement of academicians. However, for real development – practice - from those who write with the benefit of experience, is what developing nations need.

Theory and practice must go together.

I have on several occasions argued that selected Colleges of Education need to be converted to Universities of Education and/or allowed to award own degrees in various aspects of education. The teaching staff should then be subjected to the same requirements for promotion in our universities. Consequently, the quality of education at all levels in Nigeria would improve. Colleges of Education have a lot to offer this country.

Education for development is an imperative; entrepreneurship is not only necessary but critical, for even in the most advanced countries of the world businesses, mainly the small scale and medium scale are critical. This collection of well-researched papers deals with both areas, is timely, and highly recommended for all academics, students, and other stakeholders. The volume is compulsory reading for all.

Akpan H. Ekpo, PhD (Bus. Admin); PhD (Econs.)
Professor of Economics & Public Policy & Director General
West African Institute for Financial and Economic Management (WAIFEM)
Lagos, Nigeria.
June 2018

INTRODUCTION

A PERSONAL REMINISCENCE ON THE TENURE OF DR BASSEY
UBONG AND THE NEED FOR PEACEFUL CO-EXISTENCE IN NI-
GERIA

Professor Aminu Salihu MIKAILU
Chairman of the Governing Council
Federal College of Education (Technical), Omoku,
Rivers State

Introduction

I write this brief note to appreciate the efforts of Dr. Bassey
Ubong, the immediate past Provost of the Federal College of
Education (Technical), Omoku, Rivers State of Nigeria, for suc-
cessfully completing his four-year tenure on 31st March 2018.
In my capacity as the Chairman of the Governing Council of the
College that was constituted by the Federal Government in May
2017, I had the singular opportunity of working very closely
with him for almost one year. Based on my personal assessment,
I can affirm that Dr. Ubong is very reliable, humble, and highly
committed to his job both as a Chief Lecturer and as Provost/
Chief Executive Officer of the College. He was able to successfully
lead the College from the time he took control in 2014 up to
March 2018 when his tenure expired. During his tenure, the College had recorded significant progress especially in the areas of
expansion of academic programmes, physical facilities, and staff
training and development.

However, despite his achievements, resilience, good intensions,
hard work, and love for the College, he faced a lot of challenges
with respect to widespread insecurity that had engulfed Rivers

State and Omoku in particular which peaked during the last two years of his tenure (2016-2018). The absence of security during this period made the historic and bubbling town of Omoku to become a ghost of its former self as it was widely deserted resulting in a sharp fall in the number of students that were registered in the College. The level of insecurity was felt to be both political and socio-economic in nature. It was created and exacerbated by cultists, armed militias, and political thugs. It was a situation that engulfed the whole town and was therefore totally beyond Dr. Bassey Ubong's control, but which unfortunately dwarfed the scale of progress of the College from 2016 up to the end of his tenure. It is in recognition of the need for peaceful co-existence that I want to proffer some suggestions in this write up on what must be done by all the stakeholders to solve the problem of insecurity not only in Rivers State but in the entire country.

Suggestions for Peaceful Co-existence
Since the end of the Nigerian Civil War, Nigeria has witnessed many crises and conflicts. Many of these were religious, ethnic, socio-economic, and political (Bande, 1998; Albert, 1994; Anifowoshe, 2000; Nnoli, 1978; and Wakili, 2000). The crises in Kaduna, Kano, Benue, Anambra, Osun, Zamfara, Borno, Adamawa, Plateau, and Rivers States, among others, were very serious and well known. Those crises and conflicts had resulted in loss of many innocent lives. The destruction of property was also colossal. Enormous resources that could have been used to develop the country were diverted for reconstruction purposes. Economic development and educational pursuits were stalled as a result. And the image of the country was greatly battered.
Given the series of conflicts and crises that have continued to engulf the country, as well as their serious negative consequences on socio-economic, political, and educational progress, something concrete must be done to arrest the dangerous developments to ensure peaceful co-existence, stability, and socio-economic progress. Peaceful co-existence, to enrich our under-

standing, has to do with the ability of different groups within a political entity to live with one another in peace and harmony. It involves the recognition of the worth of one another and accepting of everyone as equal under the law as well as respecting the rights and privileges of one another. It also involves the recognition, understanding, and respect of each other's differences. Peaceful co-existence is central to the educational, socio-economic, and political development of any society. No real progress can take place in the absence of peace. The following few suggestions are hereby proffered for reflection and possible implementation by the stakeholders who are concerned with creation and sustenance of peaceful atmosphere in all parts of Nigeria:

1. The absence of peace in Nigeria can partly be said to have been exacerbated by the problem of the failure to prosecute and punish those who are responsible for breach of the peace. The first fundamental role of government always should be to ensure security, peace, and stability. No development can occur in the absence of peace. Therefore, those who commit crimes and promote political, ethnic, and religious violence in whatever manner should not go unpunished. Such lackadaisical attitude on the part of the authorities could only give rise to more conflicts. Not only this, people will lose faith in the government's ability to protect them and their properties, thereby forcing them to take the law into their hands which is another crime. Anarchy, lawlessness, and disorder will then become the order of the day.

2. Another factor that could affect peaceful co-existence has to do with the economic predicaments of the country. There is widespread poverty in the country, coupled with the problem of absence of transparency and accountability in almost all the tiers of government. This development has led to many people, especially the youth to become unemployed. The economic crises in the country have worsened matters. As a result, many cannot afford decent means of living. Under this circumstance, people could easily be mobilized for unlawful and selfish interests. People could be mobilized to commit crimes or generate

conflicts based on a small amount of inducement. The unfortunate thing is that this problem is becoming difficult to control because many of the leaders are not just and accountable, and therefore lack the moral courage necessary to tackle such problems.

3.   Overall, it must be emphasized that the nature and serious negative implications of crises and conflicts suggest that urgent and serious measures need to be taken to arrest the rising tides of these problems in the country. It needs to be re-emphasized that no nation can progress in the absence of peace. All Nigerians are stakeholders in the search for lasting peace in the country. But, specifically, governments at all levels should evolve effective conflict resolution mechanisms that will detect and nip in the bud potential conflicts before they erupt. As earlier indicated, the most effective way of ensuring peaceful coexistence is the punishment of offenders, once they have been identified through the due process of the law.

4.   Governments also need to seriously address the problem of unemployment and poverty in the country. This is because unemployed youths and poverty-stricken people are groups that are always susceptible to being mobilized to participate in acts capable of disrupting the peace. The behavior of our politicians and religious leaders should also be continuously monitored to ensure that they do not incite violence, thuggery, and cultism for them to capture political power or prestige. All erring politicians and religious leaders must be made to face the wrath of the law. In addition, our security and law enforcement agencies must be adequately funded and supported to enable them effectively cope with the great task of tackling crimes and insurgency throughout the country.

References
Albert, I. O. (1994). Violence in metropolitan Kano: A historical perspective. In G. O. Egahosa et. al. (Eds.). Urban violence in Africa. Ibadan: IFRA.
Anifowoshe, R. (2000). Urban violence in Nigeria: The case of

the O'dua Peoples' Congress (OPC) militia. Paper presented at the Conference on Industrialization, Urbanization, and Development in Nigeria organized by the Faculty of Social Sciences, University of Lagos, 15-16 November.

Bande, T. M. (1998). Survey of conflict in the North West Region of Nigeria. Paper presented at a conference on "Enhancing Peaceful Coexistence in Nigeria" organized by the Center for Peace and Conflict Resolution, National War College, Abuja, Giginya Hotel, Sokoto, 13th -14th May 1998.

Nnoli, O. (1978). Ethnic politics in Nigeria. Enugu: Fourth Dimension.

Wakili, H. (2000). Religious uprisings, ethnic clashes and sub-regional integration in Nigeria's northwest zone. Paper presented at the workshop on Cross-border Integration: Focusing on Nigeria's immediate Neighbors in the North-West Zone organized by the Nigerian Institute of International Affairs, and held at Giginya Hotel, Sokoto, June 27-29.

PROLOGUE

The Man of the moment
(Dr. Bassey Ubong)

CHAPTER 1

THE MAKING OF AN ENTRE-PRENEURIAL UNIVERSITY

Professor Joseph A. AJIENKA

7th Vice Chancellor
University of Port Harcourt
Nigeria

Introduction

I t should be the dream of every leader and every citizen of every nation to attain a reasonable level of socio-economic development. This is better if such development is sustainable and achieved by way of adopting best practices. Developing countries including Nigeria are beset by several challenges. These challenges can be tackled by among other institutions and agencies, universities that have the manpower and facilities for research and development of outputs of research.

Universities are specialized think-tanks of society. They are to solve problems and promote sustainable development of the nation. There are several global, national and local challenges that must be solved. Universities in Nigeria have not lived up to expectation because of peculiar challenges of funding, infrastructural deficits, and manpower gaps. From experience, even if these gaps are filled, there are still fundamental policy gaps that must be addressed. First, we need to appreciate what sustainable development is all about. There are misconceptions about sustainable development that must be clarified and then educational policies and curricular must be developed to meet it.

In Nigeria, universities engage in research; however most of them do not cooperate with industries in the effort. In many cases, the outputs of research end up in files. There is the urgent need for them to go beyond research into patenting and thereafter to commercialization. An easier route is through cooperation with business organizations and relevant government agencies. It is this cooperation and collaboration that will lead to long term development of the universities and the nation. That is the experience of most developed countries.

The University of Port Harcourt has made strong strides towards attaining the status of an entrepreneurial university. It has done this by seeking and using assistance from government and international universities and agencies, by cooperation with industry, and by best practices such as positioning by way of internal structures that promote research and development as well entrepreneurial development. Other universities need to borrow a leaf and the University of Port Harcourt needs to sustain the worthy effort for its own good and that of the nation.

Challenges On Sustainable Development

Sustainable development is development that can stand the test of time; development that can be sustained and maintained by different generations through indigenous resources, sense of beauty and knowledge cultivated on the soil, environment, and climate of the area. This is not about importing, consuming, uprooting from one place to the other or at best imitating and copying. It is not development grown from the sweat and spirit of the people in a way and manner that cannot be maintained.

After appreciating what sustainable development is, the

next thing is to redesign and develop curricular of every discipline to meet this concept. This involves having a policy of Education for Sustainable Development (ESD). To design a policy of Education for Sustainable Development, every discipline should first of all fundamentally appreciate the critical challenges facing humanity in general and at the national, regional, and local levels.

Smalley (2003) for instance describes the following ten global challenges:

1. Energy
2. Water
3. Food
4. Environment
5. Poverty
6. Terrorism and war
7. Disease
8. Education
9. Democracy
10. Population

The change from analogue to digital and the knowledge economy is also a major challenge to developing economies. At the national level with respect to Nigeria, the following major challenges can be identified:

a) Unemployment
b) Corruption
c) Poverty

These fuel kidnapping and insurgency and have deepened the fault lines (tribal and religious) that hinder development. At the local levels such as the Niger Delta, concerns about breakdown of law and order, youth restiveness, deformation of the social structure where militants have become tyrants and dictators overthrowing the leadership structure and where militants are now the nouveau riche, that is, the new rich class should be highlighted and appropriately handled.

Tackling The Challenges

Every discipline in the university, from Religious Studies, Language, to Science Education, Engineering and Management must think of how to solve the developmental problems facing the nation or at least mitigate their impact. Every lecture delivered in every discipline must address these challenges so that students imbibe the urgency of the situation. Students must be challenged to think outside the box and think creativity and innovation. They must be asked what is new all the time so that they are fully occupied by the urgent necessity; for necessity the truism that necessity is the mother of invention still holds. No Nigerian university has the structure to deal with the knowledge value chain. The main driving force in academics has been publish or perish. Consequently, we publish to become professors but with little impact on the economy, unlike professors in entrepreneurial universities such as Stanford, Harvard, Midwest Institute of Technology all in the United States of America that are closely linked with industry and have the entrepreneurial university structure to deal with innovation value chain.

In terms of university functions, we usually speak of teaching, research, and community service. We have managed to teach as if in silos in an "ivory tower." There is an evident disconnect with the realities of society. We train and graduate people for jobs that are no longer there. The economy has gone digital whereas our graduates still think analog and employment in the public and private sectors are expected to operate along the lines of digital technology. We have not equipped our graduates with the new skills for the digital age and knowledge economy. Nigerian universities must work towards giving their students entrepreneurial skills, specifically, critical thinking skills to be job creators and not employment seekers. That is the first major gap in our current educational system.

Research

As mentioned earlier, one of the problems in the university system is the publish or perish syndrome. It has led to many university teachers engaging in all kinds of unwholesome practices. The impact of scholarship on the society is not felt. Up to 2010, one is not aware of any university in Nigeria that had a Principal Officer directly involved in driving research and development (R&D) as is the global practice. No university in Nigeria has the strategic structure for research management. Such a structure must exist to:

1)   Conduct research that is locally relevant and globally recognized, the challenges of funding and poor infrastructure notwithstanding.

    a)   There must be Research Policy Documents including Research Ethics, Intellectual Property, and related issues.

    b)   There must be strategic plan for Research and Innovation with well-defined Strategic Focus and Key Performance Indicators.

2)   When research is conducted, and the output is known, this must be evaluated for beneficial impacts. We must ask what is new. What is new is discovery of new knowledge and innovation. Innovation addresses improvement in the following ways:

    a)   Productivity
    b)   Profitability
    c)   Quality
    d)   Health and wellbeing
    e)   Safety
    f)   Environmentally friendly operations
    g)   Policy
    h)   Social
    i)   Technical
    j)   Legal

Having identified what is new we must patent first before we publish. We must think of practical applications by seeking ways to bring the new to bear on the quality of life and the economy through developing new products, processes, technologies, and so on.

Therefore, the mantra must change from *publish or perish* to *patent-publish-produce* for the benefit of society. And in a knowledge economy, those who generate and apply new knowledge must enjoy the dividends of research.

Beyond Research

There is no gainsaying that several outputs of research efforts that could have been ground-breaking end up in book racks in offices. Nigerian universities have to reach out beyond research and even beyond patenting. The following stages as a follow-up to above two stages are therefore important:

3)	Industrial (technological) development - of new products in partnership with industry. We must evaluate the beneficial product value chain carefully. Pilot plants should be set up to develop, test, and validate the new prototypes, products, or software. When this is successful, it will lead to the next stage which is business development.

4)	Business Development – of licensing to corporate entities to manufacture and use or to incubate a company to start-up or spin-off. This stage involves business incubation involving venture capitalists, investors, the local Chamber of Commerce and Industry, participation in exhibitions and conferences as well as presentation to corporate bodies by way of demonstrating the benefits of the new product or service or process. The business model can also be a *joint venture*. This stage involves marketing, commercialization, and entrepreneurship to ensure market penetration of the new product.

5)	The final stage is then Town-Gown, Institute-Industry relationship of Technology Transfer, Applied Technology

Workshops (ATW), Seminars, Exhibitions, and so on, to transfer of the new knowledge and technology to industry and evaluation of the applications and competitive advantages. The products of research from "Gown" are turned over to "Town" for economic development of society. In this way a university fulfills its mandate of community service.

As earlier indicated, most research endeavours in Nigerian universities end in the laboratory and publication of papers, theses, monographs, and so on. They hardly get pass this stage. This is why there is hardly any outcomes that lead to creation of new jobs, patents, products, and new technologies.

Towards University-Industry Collaboration In Nigeria

Very often researchers complain of lack of facilities; however, the primary issue is that Nigerian academics do not have the mindset of collaborating with industry laboratories to conduct research. We do not have the orientation of applying for patents as well as evaluating and developing the results of research for purpose of application. Cooperation between universities and industry have good potentials as indicated by Adams, Chiang, and Starkey (2000)

Another implication of this is that we slave for international journals and technology scavengers. Once we sign the copyright for the journals, it is as if they have done us a favour. Very quickly, they replicate the results, apply for patents and develop the appropriate technology in technology companies. Thus, scholars make themselves intellectual slaves for others. When the products are developed we then import.

I had the personal experience of teaching new knowledge and software application in a short course. Unknown to me, in my class, was the Managing Director of a company interested in my new knowledge and technology; the person acquired everything for free. I had no patent, nothing to show for the hard work. What a big loss!

There is also the case of Dr. Ofi of Mechanical Engineering, University of Ibadan who developed a pounded yam flour machine. There was no intellectual property and he was not encouraged. Dr. Ofi struggled to commercialize his innovation. Today he is producing high quality yam flour. He retired as Professor Ofi, a former Deputy Vice-Chancellor. The University of Ibadan is not reaping the benefits of this innovation because they did not have the policy and intellectual property know-how to encourage the innovator. The intellectual slavery and drain on the economy is unimaginable. Also unimaginable are research breakthroughs that end up in files and theses because we lack the fundamental orientation and policy framework for sustainable research and development management.

The most daunting challenge to technological development it must be reiterated is the lack of synergy between industry and academia. Industrial estates are built, and industries established that simply import and export without value addition by local researchers. Most developed countries have industrial corridors in which higher institutions are fully integrated. On the other hand, major universities have science or technology or industrial parks in which the partnership with industry is consummated.

The concept of *triple helix* is the synergy and partnership between academia-industry-government. This concept assisted the development of entrepreneurial universities, and example being Stanford University in the USA working with Silicon Valley.

Way Forward

The Nigerian Government should design policies and promulgate laws to promote university-industry partnership. The Nigerian Content Policy in the oil and gas industry is one policy that is promoting local content development between industry and universities. This policy should be developed in all industries if we are to accelerate the development of the economy.

Universities must rise up to the challenge and seize the opportunities offered by becoming entrepreneurial universities. To become one there must be the following:

1)   Office of Deputy Vice Chancellor, Research and Development.

2)   Centre for Research Management.

3)   Intellectual Property and Technology Transfer Office.

4)   Strategic Research Plan with detailed research focus and direction.

5)   Research Policies, for instance Intellectual Property Policy, Licencing Policy, Research Ethics, and so on.

6)   Development of policies for International Collaboration, Industry Partnership and partnership with Government Ministries, Departments and Agencies (MDAs) such as Nigerian Content Development and Management Board.

7)   Development of policies with respect to partnership with professional bodies such as Chambers of Commerce and Industry, Bankers Committee, and others.

8)   Set up Research and Development Centres of interdisciplinary research teams.

9)   Set up Research and Development company to handle
     a) Industrial development
     b) Business development
     c) Technology Park among others

10) Strategic Research and Development Policy, Business Incubation, Entrepreneurial Centre.

11) Development and use of a curriculum of Education for Sustainable Development (ESD).

12) Set up Marketing and Communication (M&C) Unit to communicate effectively.

In taking above steps, the Legal Office must be part of Research and Development policy formulation and implementation through appropriate Memorandum of Understanding, Memorandum of Agreements and Licencing Agreements. Along above lines, the University of Port Harcourt is an important case study. The university has case studies of universities and academic innovations in Israel, a start-up nation.

The University of Port Harcourt is developing to become an entrepreneurial university by extending the concept of Triple Helix to Triple Helix Plus. That is, Government –Industry-Academia–Professional bodies partnership and collaboration with national and foreign universities. There are two extensions to the Triple Helix:

1.　　International collaboration with national and foreign universities, a policy of internationalization at home using brain gain from Nigerians in the Diaspora and academics from foreign universities.

2.　　Partnership with professional bodies for Quality Assurance/Quality Control and Professional Certification.

To develop an Entrepreneurial University, the University of Port Harcourt in 2010, created the Office of Deputy Vice Chancellor (Research and Development), set up a functional Centre for Research Management, and Intellectual Property and Technology Transfer Office. The university also developed the following Research and Development Policy documents approved by Senate:

a)　　Strategic Research Plan

b)　　Intellectual Property Document

c)　　Research Ethics Document

The implementation agency, CORDEC – Consultancy, Research, and Development Company which was involved in all kinds of business to keep afloat was refocused on developing and managing the Technology Park, Arts Village, and pilot plants (paint/allied chemicals, water plant).

The Office of Research and Development through competitive research proposals attracted:

> 1. Research Grants from Petroleum Training & Development Fund (PTDF); Tertiary Education Trust Fund (TETfund); private corporate bodies; World Bank Africa Centre of Excellence (ACE) in Oilfield Chemicals Research among others.

2. Partner Institute (PI) to Total in the Gulf of Guinea.

3. Partner Institute to Africa Virtual University in ODeL.

The Office also:

4. Reorganized Institutes and Centres.

5. Monitored Professorial Chairs.

6. Registered four patents and one licence for OPTI-WELL

7. Organized Annual Research Conference and Exhibition and coordinated participation in National Research Fairs.

8. Reorganized the School of Graduate Studies into a semi-autonomous College of Graduate School with four Schools of Graduate Studies for greater efficiency and productivity.

9. Prepared Annual Reports.

Conclusion

There is the need for universities in Nigeria to change the paradigm from publish or perish to patent-publish-produce. This will generate opportunities for job and wealth creation. There is the need for Nigerian universities to establish the structures and infrastructure to become entrepreneurial universities to contribute to sustainable development of the universities and the national economy. There is also the need for governments at the different levels to cooperate with universities; the same holds for business organizations, professional bodies, and international organizations.

References

Adams, J. D., Chiang, E. P., & Starkey, K. (2000). Industry-university cooperative research centers. *Journal of Technology Transfer*. 26 (1& 2). 73-86.

Friedman, Y. (2006). Technology transfer: Commercializing academic research. Retrieved, May 17, 2006 from http://biotech. about.com/od/licensingand techtransfer/a/techtransfer.htm.

Kankonen, E., & Nieminen, M. (1999). Modeling the triple helix from a small country perspective: The case of Finland. *Journal of Technology Transfer*. 24 (2& 3). 173-183.

Smalley, R. E. (2003). Top ten problems of humanity for next fifty years. Energy and

Nanotechnology Conference, Rice University, May 3.

CHAPTER 2

THE RELEVANCE OF POLYTECHNIC EDUCATION IN HUMAN CAPITAL DEVELOPMENT OF RIVERS STATE

Professor Addison Mark WOKOCHA
Former Registrar/Chief Executive
Teachers Registration Council of Nigeria
Abuja

Introduction

An academic with a philosophical mind hardly conducts a discourse about important concepts without the contextual Aristotelian principle. For it was Aristotle that posited the now-famous dictum: initio disputandi est definitio nominis, (For discussion to be intelligible, it must begin with definition of terms). This principle is very important especially when the terms used are not immediately self-evident in the universe of discourse.

The terms 'Human Capital Development' and 'Polytechnic Education' fall within this category. These are concise terms that need to be x-rayed to make for greater clarity and intelligibility. If these two terms are elucidated, then their interplay in the affairs of Rivers State will become not only more evident but more meaningful.

Human Capital Development

Human Capital represents the productive capacity of the people. Just like land and machinery, workers are essential requirement for production. As such, human capital denotes the skill of the labour force, how well and efficiently workers can transform raw materials and capital into goods and services. These skills – such as literacy, numeracy, cognitive and analytical skills – can be learned and honed/sharpened through education. Thus, any discussion of human capital development must touch upon education.

In fact, the link between education and economic development is realized through the labour market. Skills learned in the educational system are used by firms in the production of goods and services so that workers will be paid wages commensurate with their productivity. A further implication of this is that the educational system must not exist in a vacuum. A comprehensive study of human capital and economic development will need to consider the skills taught in the educational system, the dynamics of the labour market, and the institutions governing the means of production.

The focus of this lecture is on one of the educational subsectors for human capital development; that is the Polytechnic education. To appreciate the importance of the Polytechnic education in human capital development this lecturer intends to first expose the historical development of Polytechnics, yet it is also important say what a Polytechnic is.

What Is A Polytechnic?

Polytechnic as a generic name, refers to any non-university tertiary institution offering a variety of technical, technological/ business programmes at the National Diploma (ND) and Higher National Diploma (HND) levels. The full professional (Post-

HND) programme is also offered in some Polytechnics in Nigeria.

The central philosophy of the Polytechnic education is to impart knowledge in all branches of industrial production. It is also to impart skills in the handling of tools and materials and equip students with both theoretical and practical knowledge and experience. This concept is in tandem with National Policy on Education (NPE, 2004), which defines technical education as "that aspect of education, which leads to acquisition of practical and applied skills as well as basic scientific knowledge."

Monotechnics and Polytechnics are similar in their content, processes and products, except that monotechnics are single-subject technological institutions for specialized programmes such as agriculture, fisheries, forestry, surveying, accountancy, nursing, mining, petroleum, etc. The structure and status of their programmes shall be equivalent to those of Polytechnics. And the objectives and mode of operation of Monotechnics shall be the same as in the Polytechnics (NPE, 2004).

Historical Background Of Polytechnic Education – The International Perspective

The history of Polytechnic education dates to 1865 in Britain where Quinn Hogg began a local effort at training artisans in specific skills. The term Polytechnic was later applied to a building in Regent Street London which quickly grew into an educational institution providing knowledge and instruction in many technical subjects. It was this historical origin that shaped earlier definitions of Polytechnics as institutions aimed at promoting general knowledge, instruction skills, health and well-being (Yakubu, 2006).

The concept of Polytechnics as distinct types of educational institutions in the United Kingdom (UK) further grew out of the report of the Lord Robbins Committee on Higher Education submitted to the Government in 1963. The Policy for these institutions was outlined in a white paper entitled 'Plan for the Polytechnics and Other Colleges" released in 1966. The Polytechnics were to offer their traditional courses at the Diploma and HND/HNC levels as well as degree programmes. Initially, the Council for National Academic Awards (CNAA) awarded the degrees centrally for all Polytechnics. As the Polytechnics matured, the Government further reviewed their mission and an Act of Parliament granted them charters to award their individual degrees, thus abolishing the Council for National Academic Awards (CNAA). This is a lesson the Nigerian Governments are yet to learn and adopt.

The development of the Polytechnic system in South Africa followed the same evolutionary trend. For example, the Cape Technical College was established in 1920 and officially opened in 1923. In 1967, it was upgraded through the Technikon Act to College of Advanced Technical Education to offer tertiary education in stated field of studies. By 1993 after 26 years, the Technikon Act of 1993 empowered the Technikons (Polytechnics) to offer degrees in Technology (BTech, MTech, and DTech) (Yahani, 2006).

Concept And Growth Of Polytechnics – The Nigerian Perspective

The early promoters of Western education in Nigeria did not promote the study of sciences or technical courses which are the foundation of Polytechnic education. This was attributed to their ecclesiastic intention of using education as an instrument for proselytization and evangelization.

The first institution that had the Polytechnic concept of education was the Yaba Higher College founded in 1932. The College was subsequently moved to Ibadan to form the nucleus of the University College, Ibadan (now University of Ibadan) in 1947. Its old campus was taken over by the Yaba Technical Institute in 1948. More technical institutes were established at Enugu and Kaduna (1958), Ibadan (1960) and Auchi (1964).

The high demand for technician/technological manpower for the implementation of the 2nd, 3rd and 4th National Development Plans between 1970-85 resulted in the establishment of more colleges of technology by both Federal and State governments. The number of Polytechnics has risen rapidly from eight (8) in 1975/76 to Eighty-one (81) in 2013/2014.

The National Council on Education (NCE) adopted the no-menclature Polytechnic in 1987 to harmonize post-secondary technical education institutions offering two-year and four-year programmes leading to the award of the National Diploma and Higher National Diploma. These institutions have also diversi-fied their programmes from a handful of Diploma level courses in the 1960s to ND and HND courses in wide ranging fields of en-gineering, Education, Environmental Studies, Applied Sciences, Agricultural Sciences and Technology, Business and Financial Studies, Banking (Training NCE) and Hospitality Industrials, In-formation Communication Technology.

Establishment Of National Board For Technical Education (Nbte)

The Federal Government established the National Board for Technical Education by Act 9 of January 1977 and charged it with the responsibility of regulating Polytechnic educa-tion. In August 1985 and January 1993 respectively, the Fed-eral Government enacted Act 16 (Education National Minimum Standards and Establishment of Institutions Act) and Act 9 (Education National Minimum Standards and Establishment of Institutions (Amended/Act). With these Acts, the functions of the Board were extended to include accreditation of academic programmes in all technical and vocations Educational (TVE) in-stitutions. Act No.9 of 1ˢᵗ January 1993 further empowered the Board to recommend the establishment of private Polytechnics and Monotechnics in Nigeria.

There are at present 110 approved tertiary technical in-stitutions and 159 technical Colleges under the purview of NBTE with different types of ownership summarized in Table 1. How-ever, since the focus of this paper is on polytechnic education, a comprehensive list of approved polytechnics in Nigeria is pre-sented in Appendix 1.Table I

Summary of Number, Type and Ownership of Polytechnics, Monotechnics and Technical Colleges in Nigeria

Institution	Federal	State	Private	Total
Polytechnics	21	38	22	81
Monotechnics	23	2	2	27
Colleges of Agriculture	17	19	-	36
Colleges of Health Technology	9	40	1	50
Other Specialised Institutions	13	-	3	16
IEIs and VEIs			71	71
Technical Colleges	19	110	3	132

Source: National Board for Technical Education (NBTE) *http://www.nbte.gov.ng/history.html*

Goals Of Polytechnic Education In Nigeria

The goals of Polytechnic education, according to National Policy on Education (2004: 35) are to:

1. Provide full-time or part-time courses of instruction and training in engineering, other technologies applied science, business and management, leading to trained manpower;
2. Provide the technical knowledge and skills necessary for agricultural, industrial, commercial and economic development of Nigeria;
3. Giving training and impart the necessary skills to produce technicians, technologists and other skilled per-

sonnel who shall be enterprising and self-reliant;

4. Train people who can apply scientific knowledge to solve environmental problems for the convenience of man; and

5. Give exposure on professional studies in the technologies.

In pursuance of these goals, Government accepted to adopt the following measures:

1. to develop and encourage the ideals of Polytechnic education through students' industrial work experience; and

2. to improve immediate and long-term prospects of Polytechnic graduate and other professionals with respect to their status and remuneration.

The Polytechnics as distinct types of institution from the foregoing have been well established in Nigeria. The contributions of the Polytechnics to the economic, social, cultural and other aspects of our national development from independence (1960) to date are not easily quantifiable. The lower and middle-level manpower required by our industries, public utilities, health services, agriculture and trade are almost totally supplied by the Polytechnics. It is thus evident that the Polytechnics occupy a special place in Nigeria's overall objective of achieving technological growth and development.

Problems Of The Polytechnics/Polytechnic Education

The Polytechnic education has been fundamentally affected by several factors which pose gargantuan challenges, and which militate against the full realization of the potentials of these institutions in contributing to the development of the nation.

1. The objectives of Polytechnic education as slated by National Policy on Education (NPE 2004: 35) are laudable but the political will for their implementation leaves much to be desired.

2. Inadequate Funding has been major problem mili-

tating against effective development of Polytechnics and technical and vocational education and training (TVET) is inadequate funding. Adequate funding is crucial to the activities of the Polytechnics to enable them to:

1. Build suitable teaching facilities;
2. Employ qualified and experienced academic staff to teach the programmes;
3. Adequately equip libraries as resource centres;
4. Build suitable teaching facilities;
5. Purchase consumable materials for effective practical exercises, students' projects, maintenance work and
6. Provide adequate welfare services to staff and students (Yabani, 2006, p.18).
7. Non-Availability of Quality Teaching Staff. The non-availability in number and quality of the right caliber of academic staff is a serious militating factor to Polytechnic education. The Polytechnic sector of education in Nigeria is the only sector that has not evolved a system of producing its teachers. One may ask why it is always expected that the Polytechnics should be manned by PhD holders and Professors as Rectors yet no significant effort has been made to ensure the production of such calibre of staff from the Polytechnics education sub-sector. Is cognate experience not necessary again?

The products of engineering and other technology disciplines from the conventional universities with very limited or no work experience are not ideal for teaching programmes in the Polytechnics. It is therefore necessary to establish the principle that professional courses in the Polytechnics should be taught by holders of first or higher degrees, who had earlier passed through the ND/HND programmes because of their adequate combination of theory and practice.

8. *Stunted Academic and Professional Progression of Polytechnic Graduates*

The issue of academic and professional progression beyond

the HND is one that has caused frustration and anxiety for both staff and students engaged in Polytechnic education. The crux of the matter is whether any level or type of education in Nigeria should lead to a blind alley in the career prospects of the citizens. This is a problem that has persisted for a long time. The need to establish an acceptable procedure for the academic and professional progression of HND graduates is very urgent. The implementation of any decision to allow polytechnics to mount degree courses must be carried out systematically and without further delay.

9.   The lingering FGN/ASUP imbroglio. The Academic Staff Union of Polytechnics (ASUP) embarked on indefinite strike since the 4th of October 2013. The demands of the striking union, among others, are:

1.   the need for the constitution of governing councils for Polytechnics.
2.   non-release of white paper on the visitation panels to federal Polytechnics;
3.   commencement of NEEDs assessment of the polytechnics;
4.   continuous appointments of unqualified persons as Rectors and Provosts by some state governments;
5.   failure of government to implement the approved salary package (CONPCASS);
6.   65-year retirement age for the members;
7.   The worrisome state of some State-owned polytechnics;
8.   The continued recognition of the National Board for Technical Education (NBTE) as the regulatory body as against the union's repeated call for the establishment of National Polytechnics Commission (NPC);
9.   The non-commencement of the renegotiation of the FGN/ASUP agreement as contained in the signed agreement;
10. The snail speed on works on the amendment of the federal polytechnic Act/Scheme of Service and migration of the lower cadre to CONTISS salary scale (Nkwo,

2013, p.2).

The prolonged strike has paralyzed academic activities as well as disrupted the academic calendars of the institutions. This situation does not augur well for the scientific and technological development of the nation. Strenuous efforts should therefore be made by the parties concerned to resolve the thorny issues expeditiously. No meaningful national development can be achieved without sound and qualitative technical and techno-logical education.

The Relevance Of Polytechnic Education In Rivers State

The foregoing sections did not only give the historical per-spective of Polytechnic education but also the objectives and challenges as prelude to briefly addressing the topic: "The Rele-vance of Polytechnic Education in Human Capital Development of Rivers State." Perhaps the question to be asked should be: "Is Polytechnic Education relevant in Human Capital Development of Rivers State?" The answer is of course in the affirmative for the following reasons: The educational system in Nigeria has undergone various forms of transformation in the last few dec-ades. These transformations aimed among others at improving the education system to produce the right caliber of graduates (human capital) for national development.

In 1987 the country witnessed the birth of Polytechnic education. This is to provide employable skills for graduates and reduce high rate of unemployment. Over the years technical and vocational education and training had been limited to ap-prenticeship, vocational and technical institutions. Learning at the tertiary level had always been the acquisition of theoretical knowledge with very little hands on training. Industries had no alternative than to give their employees many weeks of 'on-the-job training.'

The Polytechnics are mandated to provide tertiary edu-cation in the field of manufacturing, commerce, sciences, tech-nology, applied sciences and arts. The polytechnics therefore have the herculean task of training graduates to fill the middle level manpower needed for industry, commerce, business and administration in the Rivers State as well as other parts of Nigeria.

The introduction of the Competency Based Training (CBT) in Polytechnic education aimed at providing graduates with employable skills should be a welcoming news to everybody in the Rivers State and must be cherished and sustained by a state which is in a hurry for accelerated development and which is endowed with abundant natural resources and also will situated for commerce and industry.

Competency Based Training (CBT) is the acquisition of appropriate knowledge, attitudes, personal trait and skills to efficiently perform work place roles in industry, commerce, management and administration.

The herald of CBT into the Polytechnic education system will provide the human capital with the necessary skills and competencies for sustainable development of the state.

The CBT suggests the 3Rs of learning:
1. Learn what is relevant.
2. Learn far more rapidly.
3. Learn for redistribution.

There is emphasis on the acquisition of basic skills and knowledge to produce desired outcome. CBT has been found to be appropriate training instrument for industry and business (Delka, 1990).

CBT emphasizes the principle of "do-it-yourself" and CBT courses are learnt in an environment that duplicates or simulates the work place (Northon, 1987).

The high points of CBT in Polytechnic education which commend it to human capital development for the state are:
1. Students require less training on the job and acquire working experience more rapidly.
2. Industrial attachment forms a major component of the programme thus graduates fit more rapidly into the job market.
3. The students develop their own learning goals and time frame and learning experiences are oriented to

continuous feedback.
4. Students develop competencies and skills for the job market.
5. Learning is flexible but challenging and does not solely depend on traditional examination to determine the progress of students.
6. Learning guide, practical manuals and readers (reference materials) are made available to students.
7. It makes the teachers prepare thoroughly and in advance and does not require detailed study of subjects that are irrelevant to the performance of professional tasks.

In sum polytechnic education is relevant to youth empowerment, economic self-reliance and societal development of the state. It will create a pool of skill-based manpower to support shop floor and field operations as the middle link between technicians and engineers in the state. The small and medium scale enterprises in the state will prefer to employ the Diploma holders because of their special skills in interpreting engineering drawings, estimating, costing, billing, supervision, measurement, testing, repair and maintenance etc. The state can indeed develop through the creation of entrepreneurs via the evolution of a sound polytechnic education policy.

Nigeria of which the Rivers State is an integral part has tried several poverty alleviation programmes to wit: Poverty Alleviation Programmes (PAP), the Directorate for Foods, Roads and Rural Infrastructure (DFFRI) the Better Life Programme (BLP) and the Family Economic Advancement Programme (FEAP) and National Poverty Eradication Programme (NAPEP).

In the Rivers State in particular, one would readily remember the Rivers State Agricultural, Agrarian Revolution of the Governor Melford Okilo administration and the School-to-Land programme of Oyakhilome administration. In 1987, the Rivers State Government launched an innovative programme dubbed the National Open Apprenticeship Scheme (NOAS) and an attempt to link education with the workplace. The scheme provided Vocational education and training to unemployed youth. It utilized facilities such as workshops and technical Instructors from private industries, government institutions and by way of subcontracting arrangements, way-side craftsman and tradesmen in the informal sector.

Under the scheme, unemployed youth and School leavers were trained for a period of 6 – 36 months under reputable Master Craftsmen. They were also taught Management, Business and administrative skills. The scheme was famed to have succeeded in training over 600,000 unemployed youth in over 80 different trades out of which about two-thirds (2/3) started their own micro-enterprises.

A mobile training scheme dubbed School-on-wheels programme introduced in 1990 was said to have provided vocational training to over 21,000 school leavers and other unskilled persons in the rural areas. The programme was of a three-month duration, after which graduates were absorbed into the National Open Apprenticeship Scheme (NOAS). Another related scheme was Waste-to-Wealth scheme under which youth were trained in the techniques of converting waste materials into useful objects. At least 8000 people were said to have been trained under that scheme.

Almost all these schemes and programmes both at the national and Rivers State levels have been discontinued for various reasons. Rivers State youth need access to both decent formal education and opportunities to acquire a range of vocational and life skills to actively participate in all spheres of an increasingly knowledge intensive society, today as young citizens and tomorrow as the state's future leaders. Unfortunately for the youth in the State acquisition of education that guarantees smooth transition from School-to-Work has been a major challenge such that many Rivers State youth end up either unemployed or underemployed in the informal sector with little protection and prospects. The difficulties of school-to-work transition would be reduced if young people acquire skills that are demanded by employers.

A more sustainable approach to human capital development in the Rivers State is through Polytechnic education that will provide training for the people in identified entrepreneurial skills and, students and trainees in science, science related and technology courses because these disciplines have natural business potentials. This can be better done in the state by expanding the courses and programmes in the Polytechnics and including foundation business courses in the science and technology curricula. Well educated and properly motivated graduates of the polytechnic would go into private business or run public business organizations more profitably than is currently the practice (Ubong, 2001).

Through TVE acquired during polytechnic education, the unemployed graduates will become productive through skill acquisition opportunities and will be able to contribute positively to the development of the state.

Skills acquisition will promote stability of the state security of life and property and balanced economic development by engaging the citizens of the state in meaningful occupational exploration and activities in areas such as agriculture, manufacturing, pottery, construction, trading, machine operations, service jobs, et cetera. By its job creation advantages, it will enhance the dignity of the people of Rivers State by making them self-sufficient and to live above the poverty level. The polytechnic education through its skills development programmes will thus provide human capital that is prepared for gainful employment and minimal unnecessary dependence.

Furthermore, salable skills in entrepreneurial activities will promote cooperative activities and better resource management through a culture of maintenance which reduces wastes and abandonment of repairable goods and equipment and thus create a healthy economic system (Okozor, 2001). The state's Internally Generated Revenue (IGR) as well as its savings will appreciate. It will also reduce the craze for rural-urban migration because effective skill acquisition will lead to rural and urban industrialization in addition to the encouragement of the establishment of Micro, Small and Medium business enterprises. Consequently, idleness and associated social and health problems will be reduced to the barest minimum in the state if the citizens are mobilized through effective and efficient polytechnic education to engage in productive ventures which will aid them into building up sound and sustainable economic base. Fraudulent practices are also likely to be reduced as the avalanche of dependents which have catalytic effect on serving officers for fraudulent activities will likely be reduced.

If salable skills are acquired by the youth of the state, certificate racketeering, forgery and production of "illiterate graduates" would be reduced along with the deleterious consequences. Besides, the unnecessary cut-throat competition for political offices as easy means of accumulating wealth and influence for continuous intimidation of other law-abiding citizens will be minimized. Political skills will abhor impunity but will be for good governance, transparency, accountability and payment of workers' salaries as and when due while the citizens of the state will share the common values of equity, respectful for one another, fairness, spirit of enterprise and integrity.

Studies of the rapid economic growth of the four "tigers" in Asia usually called the "Asian Tigers" that is, Korea, Taiwan, Hong Kong and Singapore have led to the conclusion that the basis of growth was the development of human capital (Ito, 1997; Olaleji and Abiola, 1998). It was not crude oil or other natural resources that led to their development. Wolfensohn (2000) opined that "no country has succeeded without educating its people; education is the key to sustaining growth and reducing poverty". This refers to human capital development.

There is therefore an urgent need to reform and expand the curricula of the polytechnics particularly in the Rivers State towards making the graduates to be self-reliant. This is more pressing in the case of scientists, technologists and engineers because apart from the fact that their disciplines are most adaptable to business development, Nigeria and Rivers State in particular will depend to a large extent for proper participation in the 21st century on scientists, technologists and engineers who also have adequate knowledge of managerial principles.

Inculcation of job creation skills is very necessary as government cannot provide employment for all its citizens. Since opportunities are diminishing in the country and the state young graduates must acquire skills that would give them competitive advantage over others and empower them to become job creators. There are few white-collar jobs after graduation but there are other areas youth can engage themselves depending on their areas of specialization. Embracing get-rich-quick syndrome can lead them to destruction. Rivers State youth should therefore be careful of the courses they intend to study before applying for admission into tertiary institutions.

Making Polytechnic Education Appealing

This lecturer appeals to critical stakeholders in Polytechnic Education to discontinue actions that impact negatively on the worth and dignity of polytechnic education and its products. To these ends:

1. There is need to improve the career prospects of polytechnic graduates so as not to make them appear inferior to graduates from universities. Both Federal and State governments should take the lead by:
2. Removing the GL 14 bar of holders of HND in the public service.
3. Directing the discontinuation of designating HND holders as instructors and B.Sc. holders as Lecturers in the Polytechnics – a fresh graduate, whether holders of Bachelor's degree or HND should be designated "Assistant Lecturer".
4. Allowing Polytechnics with adequate personnel and facilities to award their own degrees. Some of the notable engineering institutions in the Western World were created out of existing Polytechnics for example Henriot Watt University and Imperial College in Europe and Clarkson University in the United States of America.
5. Harmonizing admission requirements of polytechnic students with those of the students for universities.
6. Providing monetary and non-monetary incentives in the polytechnics to attract qualified and experienced teachers.
7. Urgently and effectively address the points of controversy between FGN/ASUP reminiscent of the settlement of the disagreement between FGN/ASSU.

A Special Appeal To The Rivers State Government

If Polytechnic education must continue to be relevant in the human capital development of Rivers State, then there are needs for adequate funding of Kenule Saro Wiwa Polytechnic, Bori and Captain Elechi Amadi Polytechnic, Rumuola Port-Harcourt for infrastructural and personnel development, effective pedagogical and research efforts and student and staff welfare.

Conclusion

With all hands on deck both the government of Rivers State and public spirited individuals should pool resources together to lift the tempo of polytechnic education in Rivers State. This is because of the critical role the sector can play in human capital development and entrepreneurship.

References

Delka, P. V. (1990). Skills education in business and industry: Factors for success or failure. Contractor Report, Office of Technology Assessment. United States Congress.

Federal Republic of Nigeria. Act 16 (Education National Minimum Standards and Establishment of Institutions Act.

Federal Republic of Nigeria. Act 9 (Education National Minimum Standards Establishment of Institution (Amendment) Act.

Federal Republic of Nigeria (2004). *National policy on education.* Abuja: NERDC.

Ito, T. (1997). What can developing countries learn from East Asia's economic growth. In B. Pleskovic and J. E. Stiglitz (Eds.) *Annual World Bank Conference on Development Economics.* P. 187. Washington, DC: The World Bank.

National Board for Technical Education (n.d). Summary of number, type and ownership of polytechnics, monotechnics and technical colleges in Nigeria. Retrieved, June 6, 2016 from http://www.nbte.ng/history.html

Nkwo, N (2013, November 23). ASUP Strike – the sheer neglect of polytechnic education. http://dailypost.com.ng/2013/11/23

Northon, R. E. (1987). Competency-based education and training: A humanistic and realistic approach to technical and vocational instruction. Paper presented at the Regional Workshop on Technical/Vocational Teacher Training in Chiba City, Japan. Eric: ED 279910.

Okozor, D. O (2001). Skills acquisition for sustainable poverty alleviation in Nigeria. In A. Oladimeji (Ed.). *Education and poverty alleviation in Nigeria.* Lagos: Fembis International.

Oladeji, S. A., Abiola, A. G. (1998). Poverty alleviation with economic growth strategy: Prospects and challenges. *The Nigerian Journal of Economic and Social Studies.* 40 (1). 22-28.

Ubong, B. (2001). Sustainable poverty alleviation in Nigeria through entrepreneurship education for scientists and technologists. In T. A. G. Oladimeji, et al (Eds.). *Technology education and poverty alleviation in Nigeria.* Lagos: Fembis International.

Yabani, A. M. (2006). Vision and mission of polytechnic education in Nigeria. In B. Borishade, and P. Okebukola (Eds.). *Repositioning higher education in Nigeria.* Ibadan: Heinemann Educational Books (Nig.) Plc.

Yakubu, N. A. (2006). The state of polytechnic education in Nigeria. In B. Borishade and P. Okebukola (Eds.). ibid.

Wolsfensoln, J. D. (2000). A time for action: Planning at the core of development. In H. Hinzen (Ed.). *Adult education and development.* Bonn: Institute for International Cooperation of the German Adult Education Association.

Appendix 1

Federal Polytechnics in Nigeria

S/N	Institution

1	Akanu Ibiam Federal Polytechnic, Unwana-Afikpo, Abia State
2	Auchi Polytechnic, Auchi, Edo State
3	Federal Polytechnic, Ado-Ekiti
4	Federal Polytechnic, Bauchi, Bauchi State
5	Federal Polytechnic, Bida, Niger State
6	Federal Polytechnic, Damaturu, Yobe State
7	Federal Polytechnic, Ede, Osun State
8	Federal Polytechnic, Idah, Kogi State
9	Federal Polytechnic, Ilaro, Ogun State
10	Federal Polytechnic, Kaura Namoda, Zamfara
11	Federal Polytechnic, Mubi, Adamawa State
12	Federal Polytechnic, Nasarawa State
13	Federal Polytechnic, Nekede, Owerri, Imo State
14	Federal Polytechnic, Offa, Kwara State
15	Federal Polytechnic, Oko, Anambra State
16	Hussaini Adamu Federal Polytechnic, Kazaure, Jigawa State
17	Kaduna Polytechnic, Kaduna
18	Waziri Umaru Federal Polytechnic, Birnin Kebbi, Kebbi State
19	Yaba College of Technology, Yaba, Lagos
20	Federal Polytechnic, Bali, Taraba State
21	Federal Polytechnic, Ekowe, Bayelsa State

| 22 | Federal Polytechnic, Ukana, Akwa Ibom State |

State Polytechnics in Nigeria

S/N	Institution
1	Abdu Gusau Polytechnic, Talata-Mafara, Zamfara State
2	Abia State Polytechnic, Aba, Abia State
3	Abubakar Tatari Ali Polytechnic, Bauchi
4	Adamawa State Polytechnic, Yola
5	Akwa-ibom State College of Art and Science, Numkum
6	Akwa-Ibom State Polytechnic, Ikot-Osurua
7	Benue State Polytechnic, Ugbokolo
8	Delta State Polytechnic, Ogharra
9	Delta State Polytechnic, Ozoro
10	Delta State Polytechnic, Ugwashi-Uku
11	Edo State Institute of Management and Technology, Usen
12	Gateway ICT Institute, Itori, Ewekoro, Ogun State
13	Gateway ICT Polytechnic, Igbesa, Ogun State
14	Gateway ICT Polytechnic, Saapade, Ogun State
15	Hassan Usman Katsina Polytechnic, Katsina
16	Imo State Polytechnic, Umuagwo
17	Institute of Management & Technology, Enugu
18	Jigawa State Polytechnic, Dutse
19	Kano State Polytechnic, Kano

20	Kogi State Polytechnic, Lokoja
21	Kwara State Polytechnic, Ilorin
22	Lagos State Polytechnic, Ikorodu
23	Moshood Abiola Polytechnic, Abeokuta, Ogun State
24	Nasarawa State Polytechnic, Lafia
25	Niger State Polytechnic, Zungeru
26	Nuhu Bamalli Polytechnic, Zaria, Kaduna State
27	Osun State College of Technology, Esa-Oke
28	Osun State Polytechnic, Iree
29	Plateau State Polytechnic, Barkin Ladi
30	Ramat Polytechnic, Maiduguri, Borno State
31	Rivers State Polytechnic, Bori
32	Rivers State College of Arts and Science, Rumuola, Port-Harcourt
33	Rufus Giwa Polytechnic, Owo, Ondo State
34	Sokoto State Polytechnic, Sokoto
35	Taraba State Polytechnic, Jalingo
36	The Polytechnic, Ibadan, Oyo State
37	The Polytechnic, Ijebu Igbo
38	Yobe State Polytechnic, Geidam

Private Polytechnics in Nigeria

S/N	Institution
1	Allover Central Polytechnic, Sango-Ota, Ogun State

2	Covenant Polytechnic, Aba, Abia State
3	Crown Polytechnic, Ado-Ekiti
4	Dorben Polytechnic, Bwari, FCT
5	Fidei Polytechnic, Gboko, Benue State
6	Grace Polytechnic, Surulere, Lagos State
7	Herritage Polytechnic, Ikot Udota, Eket, Akwa Ibom State
8	Igbajo Polytechnic, Igbajo
9	Interlink Polytechnic, Ijebu-Jesa, Osun State
10	Kings Polytechnic, Ubiaja
11	Lagos City Polytechnic, Ikeja
12	Lighthouse Polytechnic, Evbuobanosa
13	Nacabs Polytechnic Akwanga, Nasarawa State
14	Nogak Polytechnic, Ikom, Cross River State
15	Our Saviour Institute of Science Agric and Technology (OSISATECH), Enugu
16	Ronik Polytechnic, Lagos
17	Shaka Polytechnic, Lagos
18	Temple Gate Polytechnic Aba, Abia State
19	The Polytechnic Ile-Ife, Osun State
20	The Polytechnic Imensi-Ile
21	Tower Polytechnic Ibadan, Oyo State
22	Wolex Polytechnic, Ikeja, Lagos State

Author acknowledges the contributions of the Elechi Amadi Poly-technic, Port Harcourt to this paper.

addisonmark@yahoo.com

CHAPTER 3

BIOENTREPRENEURIAL COMPE-TENCIES AND ENGAGEMENTS IN CASSAVA WASTES-BASED COTTAGE INDUSTRIES: IMPLICATIONS FOR THE ENVIRONMENT AND SOCIO-ECONOMIC DEVELOPMENT

C. G. DIRISU; M. NWAOGU; R. DIENYE; L. A. OTOBO
Federal College of Education (Technical) Omoku, Nigeria

Abstract

Bioentrepreneurs are either entrepreneurs - originators who commercialize their scientific ideas and research results based on biological processes and systems for producing goods and services or those exploiting opportunities for marketing scientific expertise. Level of competencies for bioentrepreneurial development and commercialization of foods and industrial raw materials from cassava wastes (CW) was studied using survey design. The study sample consisted of two hundred (200) male and female adult respondents randomly selected from four communities in Rivers State, Nigeria. A structured questionnaire of 4-point Likert was developed and used in collecting data for this study. Reliability of instruments was carried out using Cronbach's alpha at 95% confidence limit with r =0.884. Data were analyzed using mean, Pearson's product moment correlation and analysis of variance (ANOVA). Results indicated that levels of entrepreneurial competencies for engagement in CW-based ventures was acceptably high ($^x > 2.5$) with male>female, although actual engagement was low for higher bioconversion (h ($^x < 2.5$). There were no significant correlations between male and female responses (r<1.00; p<0.05). Bioentrepreneurship promotes capital and job creation with attendant socio-economic gains among rural and urban dwellers in addition to fostering environmental protection and conservation. Recommendations for overcoming the bioentrepreneurship initiative bottle-necks are highlighted.

Keywords: Cassava waste; Bioentrepreneurship; Competencies, Environment, Gender, Socio-economic development.

Introduction

E ntrepreneurship is the ability and willingness to formulate, organize, and manage a business outfit either alone or with others to make profit. An entrepreneur has the ability to develop a new approach in business so as to make money (Quirk, 2003). Aside from being an originator or initiator, an entrepreneur must be willing to take risk in the process of developing a business idea.

The idea of bioentrepreneurship is borne out of the belief that a biological research and result is not just meant to be published in a journal and kept in archives but can be turned into a business by exploiting the opportunities such results can be used to create products or services for human needs (Dinglasan,

Anderson & Thomas, 2011). In the opinion of daSilva, Baydoun, and Badran (2002) advances in biological sciences offer opportunities for changing human welfare through improving the quality and quantity of healthcare and general welfare. Bioentrepreneurship is wealth creation derived from the application of the biosciences to the business context. Bioentrepreneurs look for commercial value in the technologies that they apply in conducting research in the field of biotechnology. While traditional entrepreneurs are normally involved in developing and marketing of their products, bioentrepreneurs have in-depth knowledge of the products and may also be involved in marketing it or employ marketers or team mates (Young and Mehta, 2003; Lehrer and Asakawa, 2004).

One area that bioentrepreneurs have made tremendous impact is in food biotechnology - processing crop or crop residues and transforming wastes into specialty commodities. Many food crops are being diversified for non-food purposes to provide food security as well as to meet industrial needs. One of such crops is cassava (*Manihot esculenta*). Cassava provides a reliable and inexpensive source of carbohydrate for people in sub-Saharan Africa (Hahn et al, 2010). Nigeria, Brazil, Congo Republic, Indonesia, and Thailand are among the world's major producers of cassava (Food and Agriculture Organization, FAO, 2014). Global cassava demand is on the increase because of the non-food aspect.

Cassava has diverse uses such as food for humans, animal feed, medicines, and cultural values. Cassava roots are usually peeled to remove the thin skin and leathery layer which constitutes about 15- 20% of the tuber (Onyimonyi and Ugwu, 2007). During the processing of cassava tubers into foods such as *fufu, garri,* and flour, enormous quantity of peels are generated as waste (Oboh, 2006; Ubalua, 2007; FAO, 2008). Wastewater (CWW) is also produced while cassava root sievate is obtained during *fufu* production (Figure 2). The waste peel produced currently poses a disposal problem as only a small proportion is used directly as goat feed. However, cassava residues and wastes have the potential to be an important industrial feedstock if exploited properly by biotechnological systems.

In view of above, bioentrepreneurs have mastered and perfected technologies for converting cassava wastes (and other lignocellulosic wastes) into commodities that can meet food, energy, and industrial needs. This study therefore focuses on ascertaining the competencies that male and female adults in selected urban communities in Rivers State have to facilitate entrepreneurial engagement in cottage industries. It also investigates the constraints to start up bioentrepreneurial ventures based on cassava waste technologies and highlights the implications of engagement on the socio-economic wellbeing of the people as well as their environment. The study attempted to answer the following research questions:

8. To what extent do male and female dwellers in rural-urban communities possess bioentrepreneurial competencies for economic exploitation of cassava wastes?

9. To what extent are male and female adults in urban communities engaged in entrepreneurial ventures based on cassava wastes as raw materials?

10. To what extent does bioentrepreneurial exploitation of cassava wastes affect environmental health?

11. To what extent are urban communities constrained in exploiting bioentrepreneurial potentials of cassava wastes?

Literature Review

Bioentrepreneurship, Bioentrepreneurial, Competencies, and Needs

Entrepreneurship involves generating value; it is a process of starting or building new profit-making ventures, and the process of making available new products or services. Lehrer and Asakawa (2004) used the term, "science entrepreneurship" to mean the simultaneous dedication of scientists to academic science and economic profit, that is, focusing on commercialization of scientific discoveries. One of such areas of commercial application of science is in biotechnology, which is the use of biological organisms and systems for bioindustry. A person in such venture can be termed a bioentrepreneur. Turning biological science products into business usually takes place when a scientist or an individual discovers a pathway or mechanism in biology that can fetch money. A bioentrepreneur is the inventor of a business or one who perceives the market need for the product or service based on biological processes and systems (Mehta, 2004). In the latter case, the bioentrepreneur recognizes the market needs of his/her invention/product and builds a business to exploit that opportunity (Blank, 2013).

Bioentrepreneurship may mean starting up a new business using biological principles and skills. It exists when a person develops a new approach to an old business or idea. The bioentrepreneur like other entrepreneurs must be able to recognize opportunity, which culminates in ensuring that his/her perception of the relationship between the invention and the final product is refined into a business model that will explain how the industry will create wealth or product for other people that would like to invest in the business (Mehta, 2004). They launch their products with a business model of forming a fully integrated industry or company. Bioentrepreneurs background is as diverse as individuals in any other fields.

A key ingredient in a successful entrepreneurship is self-knowledge. Bioentrepreneurs must know their strengths and weaknesses and exhibit high levels of certain competencies. Bioentrepreneurial competencies are part of scientific/ biotechnological skills, life skills as well as managerial skills which equip the bioentrepreneur to succeed. They include occupational /vocational skills and capabilities that enable an individual to make economic gains (Dirisu, 2017). The competencies expected of a bioentrepreneur will include decision making, creativity and innovation as well as critical thinking, team work and networking. To be able to harness waste resources and convert same into valuable products and or start up cottage industries requires that the bioentrepreneur be knowledgeable in the product and production process. Such an individual is also expected to be competent in coping with stress and challenges of business.

Possession or development of bioentrepreneurial competencies enables the individual to the able to self-manage, solve problems, and understand the biologically-based business environment, and work well as part of a team in the production process, which always have diverse steps. He or she is also able to manage time and people, and in some cases collaborates with big companies or wealthy company owners to start up, providing the scientific ideas, principles, and description of the production process (Baron and Shane, 2004; Lehrer and Asakawa, 2004).

Model/Process For Bioentrepreneurship Creation

The process for creating a new bioentrepreneurship business involves five processes: recognizing the opportunity for the product or service; acquiring/securing the intellectual property (IP) right which may involve licensing; funding; development of the product technology which is based on research; and ensuring the survival of the business through additional funding, collaborations, and so on. The entrepreneur is either the inventor of the product/technology or initiator/founder of the business or the one who perceived the market need of the new technology/product and started the business of marketing of the service/product. (Mehta, 2004). The competencies and needs of the bioentrepreneur (either the technopreneur/scientific entrepreneur or the market perceiver) are summarized in Table 1.

Table 1
Some Competencies Requirements for (Bio)Entrepreneurship Processes

Bioentrepreneurial venture stage	Bioentrepreneur /Technopreneur required competencies
Recognize opportunity	Solid understanding of and expertise in specific, well-characterized technology (Intellectual Property, IP)
	Established credibility with peers, investors and customers.
Secure IP rights	A strong position to easily license his/her own invention from the university into the startup. and company executive. Need to have an understanding of future IP needs
Fund team and build company	Strength in early phases of company, where main efforts are on research and most of the personnel are technically oriented.

41

Develop tech-nology to product	Needs experience of commercial product development, particularly issues in scaling up. Unbiased perspective to evaluate the technology's realistic potential versus its elegance.
Survive	Needs to understand that his or her appropriate position within growing company may not be at the helm, but in a specific technical leadership position or on the Scientific Advisory Board.
Market	Needs to shift focus from developing technology to building a strong commercial team speedily and efficiently.

Adapted from Mehta (2004)

Entrepreneurship Opportunities For The Life Sciences

Some bioentrepreneurship opportunities based on biology or life sciences which people can initiate and startup are listed in Table 2. The scientific principles or theories are usually applied hence the bioentrepreneur is expected to be well versed with the details of the business.

Table 2
Diversity of Bioentrepreneurship Venture Opportunities

	Bioentrepreneurship Opportunities	Economic Importance/Value
1	Biofuel (bioethanol, biogas, biodiesel) production from agro and industrial wastes by microbial fermentation	Wealth creation by sale of products, environmental pollution control
2	Bee keeping	Honey collection for sweetening or as industrial raw materials and also bee wax.
3	Aqua culture	Fish farming. prawn farming and crab culture – protein source
4	Sea weed culture and sea weed farming	Products include agar, agarose, machines, thickening agents.
5	Floriculture	Growing flowers for ornamental values

		and for export as well as for domestic market.
6	Horticulture	Growing fruits and vegetable which can be sold in the market local or exported
7	Botanical garden and zoo/ animal park	For ecotourism- generates money and for educational research
8	Aquarium	For research and sales.
9	Mushroom culture	Mushroom are meat substitute and have good export market value
10	Water Conservation	For agriculture and drinking
11	Tree planting	Preservation of soil fertility and prevention of spreading of the desert; Biological methods are having advantage over the others
12	Poultry farming	rearing birds used for human consumption
13	Bioinsecticide production	To control insect pests to increase agricultural yield.
14	Food fermentation e.g. *ogi, ogiri, dawadawa,* yoghurt	Food preservation, Food fortification with vitamins
15	Serology	Blood typing, diagnostic laboratory services
16	Conservation of medicinal plant	Herbal health products for control of infection and diseases

Adapted from daSilva et al (2002); Ejijibe (2012)

Bioentrepreneurial Potentials Of Cassava Wastes For Industrial Applications

Cassava wastes be it solid or liquid is valuable feedstock for industrial production as listed in Table 3.

Table 3
Composition of Cassava Wastewater and Bioentrepreneurship Potential Applications

Cassava waste content	Industrial Application	Reference
Microorganisms	Lactic acid bacteria. Food fermentation	Arotupin (2007) Ebabhi et al (2013)
	Yeasts can be used for bread making, brewing for alcohol production	
Organic acid	Lactic acid is used in food preservation	Odunfa (2005)
Amino acid	Lysine	Oboh (2006), Odunfa (2005)
Enzymes'	Amylase is used as additives for removing starch from textiles, liquefaction of starch	Haki, G.D. and S.K. Rakshit, (2003) Arotupin (2007)
	Formation of dextrin in baking	
	Preparation of high fructose corn syrup	
	Saccharification of starch for brewing	Aiyer, 2004)
	Cellulase is used for crushing apples to increase yield of juice	Bhat (2003)
	Colour brightener in textile industries	Csizer et (2001)
	Making stone wash jean in jeans	Haki and Rakshik (2003)
	Paper processing	Logen corporation (2003)
Peels, pellet, leave	Poultry feed (birds and goat feed)	Oboh (2002); Fasuyi (2005), Morgan and Choct (2016), Nwoko et al (2016)
Peel, wastewater	Bioethanol production	Ohimain (2010), Adelekan (2012); Adiotomre (2015); Nuwamanya et al (2012), Ezebuiro et al, 2015; Chibuzor et al, 2016).
	Bioremediation of crude oil polluted soil	Romanus et al, 2015).

Methodology

Study Design: The survey design was used along with personal interviews in to seek opinions from a defined population on the level of utilization of cassava wastes in selected urban communities in Rivers State, Nigeria.

Study Population and Sample: The population of the study covered four communities in four local government areas (LGAs) in Rivers State. These include Omoku in Ogba/Egbema/Ndoni LGA; Ahoada in Ahoada East LGA; Choba and Ozuoba in Obio-Akpor LGA; and Elele and Emuoha in Emuoha LGA. 200 hundred adult respondents were randomly selected and used for the study. Respondents were distributed as shown in Table 4.

Table 4

Distribution of Respondents (by Gender) used for Bioentrepreneurship Competencies and Engagement Survey

Local Government Area (LGA)	Community	No. of Respondents by Sex	
		Male	Female
Ogba/Egbema/Ndoni	Omoku	3	17
	Okwuzi	5	15
	Obite	2	18
Ahoada-East	Ahoada	7	12
Obio-Akpor	Choba	8	22
	Ozuoba	10	21
Emuoha	Elele	9	21
	Emuoha	10	20
	Total	54	146

Source: Field Work

A structured questionnaire of 4-point Likert scale was developed and used in collecting data for this study. The reliability of the instrument was determined by Cronbach's Alpha with a reliability coefficient of 0.883, which was rated highly reliable for obtaining information from respondents. The questionnaires were administered and retrieved on the spot through a Research Assistant. Data collected were analyzed using mean to score the responses. Any item in the question with a mean response of >2.5 was retained or accepted, while any item with mean response < 2.5 was not regarded and rejected. Data was analyzed using Pearson's Product Moment Correlation and one-way analysis of variance (ANOVA) to determine correlation and significant differences between male and female responses at 0.05 alpha level.

Results

Level of Entrepreneurial Competencies for Cassava-Waste Bioconversion Technologies

Both gender groups had acceptably high level of competencies (^{X}>2.5) except for good networking. Females had lower competency for risk management than males. Male respondents had higher competencies for bioentrepreneurship involving bioconversion of CW into wealth. There was however no significant difference in the level of bioentrepreneurial competencies for both gender groups as indicated by single factor analysis of variance, $F(1,16)=0.493,p0.235>0.05$ (Table 5). There was also no significant correlation between male and female responses ($r=0.845,p>0.05$).

Table 5
One-way Analysis of Variance on Bioentrepreneurial Competencies by Gender

Sources	SS	Df	MS	F	P value	F crit	RMSSE	Omega Sq
Between Groups	0.0	1.00	0.04017	0.496016	0.49138	4.493998	0.234761	-0.02881
Within Groups	1.3	16.00	0.080985					
Total	1.3	17.00	0.078584					

Entrepreneurial Engagement in Cassava Waste-based Industry by

Gender

Cumulative mean engagement of females was slightly higher than that of male respondents (X=2.4>2.6). Engagements in higher biotechnological processing had lower mean (<2.5) and hence rejected, which implies that conversion of cassava wastes into such valuable products were done to a small extent. There was no significant difference in both gender responses on bioentrepreneurial engagement in cassava waste based cottage industries, $F(1, 14=0.84; p0.37>0.05)$ (Table 6).

Table 6
One-way Analysis of Variance on Bioentrepreneurial Engagement by Gender

Sources	SS	df	MS	F	P value	F crit	RMSSE	Omega Sq
Between Groups	0.227	1	0.227	0.84	0.375	4.60 011	0.32	-0.01
Within Groups	3.786	14	0.27					
Total	4.013	15	0.268					

Impact Of Non-Cassava Waste Utilization And Biotransformation On The Environment

Mean responses are well above the cutoff level of 2.5, indicating that solid and liquid wastes derived from cassava processing for food were perceived to impact negatively on the environment. Male and female responses were not significantly correlated ($r=0.728; t=1.63>0.05$). There was also no significant difference in the mean responses by gender in their perceived impacts, $F(1, 8) =2.308, p0.17>0.05$ (Table 7)

Table 7
ANOVA Statistic on Perceived Environmental Impacts of Cassava Wastes

Sources	SS	df	MS	F	P value	F crit	RMSSE	Omega Sq
Between Groups	0.026319	1	0.026319	2.30827	0.1671 72	5.31 7655	0.679451	0.115691
Within Groups	0.091217	8	0.011402					
Total	0.117536	9	0.01306					

Constraints to Cassava waste Bioentrepreneurship Engagement in Cottage Industries

Mean responses ranged from 2.0 to 3.2 for males and from 2.0 to 2.9 for females. Among the constraining factors raised, only lack of education was not considered as a factor for low engagement in cassava wastes-based entrepreneurship business. There was significant correlation between males and females in their responses (r= 0.98; t(0.006<0.05). ANOVA statistic on mean responses was not significant, F(1,12)- 1.557; p0.23>0.05 (Table 8).

Table 8
ANOVA Statistic on Mean Bioentrepreneurship Engagement Constraints by Gender

Sources	SS	df	MS	F	P value	F crit	RMSSE	Omega Sq
Between Groups	0.248118	1	0.248118	1.557112	0.23589	4.747225	0.47164	0.038271
Within Groups	1.912142	12	0.159345					
Total	2.16026	13	0.166174					

Discussion

Entrepreneurial skills and attitudes provide benefits to humanity even beyond their application to business activity. Ismail et al (2011) state that successful entrepreneurship is achieved if the entrepreneur has vision, is innovative, has passion for the business, can identify opportunity, create value out of nothing, and ensure growth of the business. Competencies relevant to entrepreneurship are creativity and innovation. In Figure 3, bioentrepreneurial competency levels of both male and female respondents (x >2.5) was not significantly different (Table 5). In the opinion of daSilva et al (2002) and Ejijibe (2012) establishment of biotechnology farms and commercialization of biology education could be a means for money making and job creation, which is the main essence of entrepreneurship.

Akpomi (2008) also holds that relevant technical and business skills need to be provided to those who choose to be self-employed and/or to start their own ventures. Dirisu (2016) highlighted life skills which can be engaged in promoting health. Bioentrepreneurial engagement in cassava wastes-based ventures were higher among females than males as shown by this study (Figure 4) although low engagement was observed for businesses involving more biotechnological production that use microorganisms and microbiological techniques (x <2.5). There were higher engagements in starch and feed than bio-chemicals or biofuel production. This finding is in line with Elias, Rival, and Mickey (2000) and Hahn and Keyser (2006). Cassava is mainly cultivated for food for most people across the world, particularly sub-Saharan Africa, South America, and Asia; and women are more engaged than men in cassava processing (Smith et al, 2001; Okorji, Eze, & Eze, 2003). In Figure 3, weighted mean score of respondents was below 2.5 and hence rejected, which implies that conversion of cassava wastes into valuable products were done to a small extent. Most people in West Africa see cassava peels and other wastes as materials to be thrown away rather than a potential resource.

This is supported by Adebayo et al (2008), Adelekan (2010) and Ibeto, Okoye, and Efeofule (2014).The use of cassava wastes as feedstock for industrial production have been reported for biogas and bioethanol (Ezebuiro et al, 2000; Adesanya et al, 2008; Nuwamanya, Chiwona-Karltun, Kawuki, & Baguma 2012; Sarker, Ghosh, Bannerjee, & Aikat 2012; Adiutomre, 2015), mushroom (Dirisu et al, 2016), improved animal feed (Morgan and Choct, 2016) as well as biodegradation and bio-remediation of crude oil polluted soil (Romanus et al, 2015). (Table 2). Economic situation however forces some people to use some cassava waste products as food such as starch and cassava grit. The use of cassava peels as animal feed is because it has a high level of nutrients including carbohydrates (Nwoko, Enyin-naya, Okolie, & Nkwoada 2016). Drying, boiling, and fermenta-tion are known to reduce the cyanide content, which is an anti-nutrient compound in the cassava, to non-toxic levels (Oboh, 2002; Oliveira, Reis, & Nozaki 2001; Fasuyi, 2005; Odunfa, 2005;

FAO, 2014). CWW have also been used as biofertilizer by farmers who may not have access to inorganic fertilizers and as herbicides (Ogundola and Liasu, 2007; FAO, 2008). Also, enzymes such as amylase and cellulase have been produced from microorganisms particularly yeasts found in CWW (Aiyer, 2004; Haki and Rok, 2003; Ladeira et al, 2015). Both enzymes have industrial applications (Arotupin, 2007) (Table 3).

In Figure 5 mean score for all items was > 2.5, which implies that cassava wastes impacted the environment and people negatively when improperly managed. Accordingly, to Smith et al (2001), the disposal of agricultural wastes on land and into water bodies are common, among local processers and have been of serous ecological and health hazards. Cassava is known for its high levels of cyanogenic glucosides ((Ngiki et al., 2014), which is responsible for its toxicity (Oti, 2002; Fasuyi, 2005). Unsustainable disposal results in the pollution of both water and land resources, increase in rodents and insect vector diseases thereby creating public health concerns. Besides not getting additional source of income from adding value to cassava peels, heaps of cassava peels or accumulation of CWW affects the aesthetic beauty of the environment with offensive odours in the dump sites.

In Figure 6, it can be observed that weighted mean score was above 2.5 even though more respondents rejected the fact that lack of education and inadequate supply of electricity did not affect ability of respondents to convert cassava wastes into valuable products. Other constraints reported are poor scientific and technical know-how; lack of professional managers and processing equipment; and poor financial management. These can hinder engagement in bioentrepreneurship ventures as supported by daSilva et al, 2002; FAO, 2008; Ejijibe, 2015).

Implications Of Wastes-Based Entrepreneurship Engagement

1. Environmental and health protection: Investment in bioentrepreneurship ventures using agro-industrial wastes or

crop residues serve as substrates or feedstock for bioconversion. This does not only ensure that food and economic crops are preserved or conserved but also enhances environmental integrity by minimizing pollution and hence infections due to their improper disposal of wastes. Biofuels derived from cassava (and other lignocellulosic wastes) are pollution free and pose little or no environmental threat, cause no climate changes, and the by-product of fermentation can be used as animal feedstock.

2. Wealth creation and economic development: Entrepreneurs are key players in the biotechnological or biology-based business culture of any nation and are involved in creating wealth and jobs which enhance economic growth particularly in agriculture, breweries, food and medical and health industries. The profits that accrue to bioentrepreneurs and payments for labour and marketers, machines, raw materials and buildings by the entrepreneur can increase the national income and by extension, standard of living. It is reported that rural women in Africa as for example, Burkina Faso process shea butter and have established direct links in global markets (DaSilva et al, 2002).

3. Employment creation: Bioentrepreneurs create small businesses by employing local or non-school citizens to engage in some or part of the production and sale process with a monthly wage. For example, people are employed in the processes of cassava peeling, washing, grating/grinding, bagging, frying, and sale of final product (*garri*). For the utilization of cassava wastes or wastewater, people can be hired to source for and collect the wastes or kiosks can be established where residents supply their wastes to the cottage industry and collect rewards or money. The labour intensive nature of small businesses enables them to create more jobs than the big businesses.

4. Improvement in the standard of living: The introduction of high quality goods and services can transform lives of people in both rural and urban communities. The importance of fermented food in health must be recognized.

5. Reduction in rural-urban migration: Promotion of bioentrepreneurship can reduce rural-urban drift to cities in search of white-collar jobs.

6. Development of local biotechnological base: Globally, indi-

genous biotechnological development has been evolved by indigenous bioentrepreneurs. For example, bread making, wine and alcohol production, condiments, enzyme, food additives production started from traditional fermentation processes. This helps in technology transfer for rapid economic growth in a nation.

Conclusion And Recommendations

Results of this study indicate that males had higher competencies than females for engaging in bioentrepreneurial ventures involving cassava wastes industries. Conversion of cassava wastes into biotech products occurred to a small extent. Cassava waste products affect the environment and people negatively but converting them into useful products minimizes environmental pollution and enhances environmental protection and conservation. It also creates wealth and job opportunities which enhances the socio-economic wellbeing of rural-urban populations. There were some constraints to conversion of cassava waste products into valuable products. Based on the results, it is hereby recommended that technologies that encourage the utilization of cassava peels for beneficial uses to both human beings and animals should be emphasized by research institutes. Training should be organized for cassava processors on the use of cassava peels to produce mushroom and biogas as well as animal feeds.

References

Adebayo, A. O., (2008). Using cassava waste to raise goats. Project 2008-4345. World Bank Development Marketplace.

Adelekan, B. A. (2010). Investigation of ethanol productivity of cassava crop as a sustainable source of biofuel in tropical countries. *African Journal of Biotechnology.* 9 (35). 5643-5650.

Adewale, J. G. (2009). Effectiveness of non-formal education programs in Nigeria: How competent are the learners in life skills? *Australian Journal of Adult Learning.* 49 (1). 191-206.

Aiyer, P. V. D. (2004). Effect of C.N ratio on alpha amylase production by *Bacillus licheniformis* SPT 27. *African Journal of Biotechnology.* 3. 519-522.

Akinrele, I. A. (2008). The manufacture of *garri* from cassava in Nigeria. Proceedings of First International Congress in Food Technology, London. pp. 633-644.

Akpomi, M. E. (2008). Developing entrepreneurship education programme (EEP) for higher educational institutions (HEIs) in Nigeria. Post-doctoral research project carried out at the University of Reading, Reading, United Kingdom.

Arotupin, D. J. (2007). Evaluation of microorganisms from cassava waste water for production of amylase and cellulase. *Research Journal of Microbiology.* 2. 475-480. Doi: 10.3923/jm.2007.475.480.

Baron, R., & Shane, S. (2004). *Entrepreneurship: A process perspective.* Ohio: South-Western Press.

Bhat, M. K. (2000). Cellulases and related enzymes in biotechnology. *Advanced Biotechnology.* 18. 355-383.

Blank, S. (2013). Reinventing life science startups: Evidence-based entrepreneurship. Retrieved, November 24, 2014 from https://www.forbes.com/sites/steveblank/2013/08/20/reinventing-life-science-startups-evidence-based-entrepreneurship/#2d51e6d99950

Csizar, E., Losonczi, A., Szakacs, G., Rusznak, I., Bezur., L., & Reicher, J. (2001). Enzymes and chelating agent in cotton pretreatment. *Journal of Biotechnology.* 89. 271-279.

daSilva, E.J., Baydoun, E., & Badran, A. (2002). Biotechnology and the developing world. *Electronic Journal of Biotechnology.* 5 (1). 64-92. Doi: 10.2225/vol5-issue1-fulltext-

Dinglasan J. A., Anderson, D. J., & Thomas, K. (2011). Scientific entrepreneurship in the materials and life science industries. *Methods Molecular Biology.* 726. 379-91. Doi: 10.1007/978-1-61779-052-2_24.

Dirisu, C. G. (2017). Life skills for adult and non-formal education: Meaning, scope, importance and applications. A paper delivered during Workshop on Adult and Non-Formal Education: Implication for Community Development in OML

58 Areas of TEPNG at Obite, Rivers State, Nigeria 17-18th march, 2017. Workshop Proceeding, pp 20-33

Ebabhi, A. M., Adekunle, A. A., Okunowo, W. O., & Osuntoki, A. A. (2013). Isolation and characterization of yeast strains from local food crops. *Journal of Yeast and Fungal Research* 4(4). 38-43. Doi: 10.5897/JYFR2013.0112.

Ebabhi1, A. M., Adekunle, A. A., Okunowo, W. O., & Osuntoki, A. A. (2013). Isolation and characterization of yeast strains from local food crops *Journal of Yeast and Fungal Research* 4(4). 38-43. Doi: 10.5897/JYFR2013.0112

Ejilibe, O. C. (2012). Entrepreneurship in biology education as a means for employment *Knowledge Review.* 26 (**3**). 84-96.

Elias, M., Rival, L., & Mickey, D. (2000). Perception and management of cassava *(Manihot Esculenta)* diversity among Makushi Amerindians of Guyana (South America). *Journal of Ethnobiology* 20(2): 239-265.

Food and Agriculture Organization (2008). Existing cassava processing/environment knowledge base. Retrieved, May 12, 2018 from http://www.fao.org/docrep/007/y2413e/y2413e0e.htm

Food and Agricultural Organization (2014). *Food outlook.* Biannual report on global food markets. Rome: Food and Agricultural Organization.

Fasuyi, A. O. (2005). Nutrient composition and processing effects on cassava leaf (*Manihot esculenta*) anti-nutrients. *Pakistan Journal of Nutrition* 4 (1).37-42.

Hahn, S. K., & Keyser, J. (2006). Cassava as basic food of Africa. *Outlook on agriculture* 4. 95-100.

Hahn, S. K. (2010) Cassava end African crisis. In: Tropical root crops-root crops and the African food crisis; pp 24-29

Haki, G. D., & Rakshit, S. K (2003). Development in industrially important thermostable enzymes: A review. *Bioresources.* 89. 17-34.

Ibeto, C. N., Okoye, C. O. B., Ofoefule, A.U. (2014). Bioethanol production from thermally pre-treated corn chaff and cassava waste water. *Int'l Res J Pure Appl Chem* 4: 227-233.

Martin, L. (2014). The importance of life skills-based education. Retrieved June 10, 2018 from http://www.learningliftoff.com/the-importance-of-life-skills-based-education/#.WKH2glXyvIU>

Mehta, S. (2004). Paths to entrepreneurship in the life sciences entrepreneurship. doi:1038/bioent831]. Retrieved, June 10, 2018 from https://www.nature.com/bioent/2004/041001/full/bioent831.htmlEnrepreneurs

Morgan, N. K., Choct, M. (2016). Cassava: Nutrient composition and nutritive value in poultry diets. *Animal Nutrition.* 2. 253-261

Nuwamanya, E., Chiwona-Karltun, L., Kawuki, R. S., & Baguma, Y. (2012). Bio-ethanol production from non-food parts of cassava (Manihot esculenta) AMBIO 41. 262–270. Doi 10.1007/s13280-011-0183-z

Nwoko, C. I., Enyinnaya, O. C., Okolie, J. L., & Nkwoada, A. (2016). The proximate analysis and biochemical composition of the waste peels of three cassava cultivars. *International Journal of Scientific Engineering and Applied Science.* 2 (11). 64-99.

Oboh, G., Akindahunsi, A.A., & Oshodi, A. A. (2002). Nutrient and anti-nutrient content of *Aspergillus niger* fermented cassava products flour and garri. *Journal of Food Component Analysis.* 15. 617-622.

Oboh, G. (2006). Nutrient enrichment of cassava peels using a mixed culture of Saccharomyces cerevisae and Lactobacillus spp. solid media fermentation. *Electronic Journal of Biotechnology*, 9 (1): 46-49.

Oduah, A. A., Dirisu, C. N. G., & Egbule, O. (2014). Mushroom production from organic wastes. *GIRD International Journal of Science and Technology.* 2 (1). 215-221.

Odunfa, S. A. (2005). African fermented foods. *Microbiology of fermented foods*, pp 155-162. Amsterdam: Elsevier Applied Science.

Ogundola, A. F., & Liasu, M. O. (2007) Herbicidal effects of effluent from processed cassava on growth performances of *Chromolaena odorata* weeds population. *African Journal of Biotechnology.* 6 (6). 685-690.

Okorji, E.C., Eze, C. C., & Eze, V. C. (2003). Efficiency of cassava processing techniques among rural women in Owerri, Imo State, Nigeria. ASR 3 (2). 84-96.

Okunade, D. A., & Adekalu, K. O. (2013). Physiochemical analysis of contaminated water resources due to cassava wastewater effluent disposal. *European International Journal of Science and Technology.* 2 (6). 75-85.

Oliveira, M.A., Reis, E.M., & Nozaki, J. (2001). Biokinetic parameters investigation for biological treatment of cassava mill effluents. *Water, Air, and Soil Pollution* 126 (3-4). 307-319.

Osunbitan, J. A. (2012). Short term effects of cassava processing waste water on some chemical properties of loamy sand soil in Nigeria soil. *Journal of Soil Science and Environmental Management.* 3 (6). 164-171.

Oti, E. E. (2002). Acute toxicity of cassava mill effluent to the African catfish fingerlings. *Journal of Aquatic Science.* 17. 31-34.

Oyeleke, S. B., Duada, B. E. N., Oyewole, O. A., Okoliegbe, I. N., & Ojebode, T. (2012). Production of bioethanol from cassava and sweet potato peels. *Advanced Environmental Biology.* 6 (1). 241-245.

Sarkar, N., Ghosh, S. K., Bannerjee, S., & Aikat, K. (2012). Bioethanol production from agricultural wastes: An overview. *Renewable Energy.* 37. 19-27.

Ubalua A.O. (2007). Cassava wastes: Treatment options and value addition alternatives. *African Journal of Biotechnology.* 6 (18). 2065-2073.

Young, N., & Mehta, S. (2004). The social structure of innovation. Paper presented at Lally-Severino ENI Symposium on the Intersection of Entrepreneurship, Networks, and Innovation, Troy, New York, October 2–3, 2003.

Acknowledgments

The authors wish to thank Ms. Benita for administering and retrieving the completed questionnaire used for the survey.

chimezie.dirisu@fcetomoku@edu.ng

CHAPTER 4

THE ROLE OF AGROFORESTRY IN THE SOCIO-ECONOMIC DEVELOPMENT OF HOUSEHOLDS IN OKIGWE ZONE OF IMO STATE, SOUTH EASTERN NIGERIA

Nnamdi C. CHIBO
I. E. OSUMGBOROGWU
Nnamdi Oriachor JAMES
Department of Geography and Environmental Management
Imo State University, Owerri

Abstract

The study investigated the contributions of agroforestry in Imo State to find out its relevance in the socio-economic development of the study area. 450 copies of questionnaire were distributed in three local government areas; 433 copies were retrieved representing 96.2%. The result revealed that agroforestry is an economic activity in the study area but not a major one; that it is practiced by more males than females (although there are more women than men in non-timber forest products) and by more of the people of above 55 years of age than the other age groups. The study however concluded that agroforestry can boost to the economy of Imo State if there is adequate investment and commitment by the government of the day and attitudinal change among individual farmers. Recommendations included education and research as well as policy reform.

Keywords: Agroforestry; Non-Timber Forest Products (NTFPs); Socio-economic Development; Poverty; Investment.

Introduction

Notwithstanding the enormous revenues from oil, some of the factors fueling the continuous economic stagnation in Nigeria, particularly in Imo state centre on the neglect of renewable natural resources sector, such as agriculture and forestry. Nigeria ranks among the most enterprising nations in Africa and her potential as an exporter of agro-industrial products and manufactured goods draws major interests from international investors.

Nigeria accounts for 54% of West African population and 51% of its gross national product. Crude oil generates about 80% of the foreign reserves and 10.6% of Gross Domestic Product (GDP) at factor cost (Merem, 2005). Apart from oil, agriculture is still the activity of majority of Nigerians, constituting about 40% of GDP. While the current policy framework emphasizes the development of non-oil sector especially agriculture, Nigeria's agriculture faces a set of challenges common across sub Saharan Africa such as limited capital, small land holdings, declining soil fertility, massive deforestation and unsustainable land use practices (WTO, 2004).

Nigeria was once covered by a variety of vegetation in the humid tropical rainforest in the south and savannah in the north. Much of these luxuriant forests in the south, including Imo state, have been cleared by pressures mounted by human activities. The areas cleared are used to produce various agricultural products including crop and forestry products. Generally, the southern rainforest is a source of the country's timber resource as well as oil palm produce. The forests of Imo State provide above two commodities in addition to African breadfruit (*Treculia africana*); local star apple *(chrysophylum albidum); ube (dacryodes edulis);* para-rubber *(Hevea brazilienesis);* some fruit crops such as plantain, banana *(Musa species),* pineapple, cashew and others. There are also non-timber forest products (NTFPs) such as *ukpa (Tetracapidum conophorum); utazi (Gongronema latifolia); okazi (Gnetum africana); uziza (Piper guineensis)* among others. These products contribute in one way or the other to socio- economic development of the area.

Currently, the tropical rain forest which is a source of these products that cover about two percent of the total land area of Nigeria is being depleted at an annual rate of 3.5 percent. The annual rate of change in total forest area from 1990-2000 stood at 4.0 million hectares (Central Intelligence Agency, 2000; Food & Agricultural Organization, 2001; Mantu, 2001; United Nations Environmental Project, 2003). Agroforestry systems can be advantageous over conventional agriculture and forest production methods through increased productivity, social returns and ecological goods and services provided. Biodiversity in agroforestry systems is typically higher than in conventional agricultural systems.

Statement Of The Problem

Deforestation is a problem in Imo State of Nigeria. However, are general socio-economic problems in the area including food security which agroforestry should ameliorate. It is therefore necessary to attempt to find out if agroforestry has been contributing to the socio-economic well-being of the people of the study area.

Objectives Of The Research

The overall aim of this research is to demonstrate whether agroforestry makes an important contribution to the economic and social development of Imo State. The specific objectives are to:

(i)   Document the major agroforestry practices and products in the study area.

(ii)   Determine whether agroforestry has positively affected, stimulated, or adversely affected the socio-economic development of the study area, and in effect Imo State.

(iv)   Identify the relationship between agroforestry and other economic activities.

The Study Area

The study area for this research is Imo State with searchlight on Okigwe, Isiala Mbano, and Onuimo Local Government Areas. Imo State is one of the states in the south eastern part of Nigeria. It is located within the tropical rain forest zone of the country. It lies between latitudes 5° 10'N- 6° 00'N and longitude 6° 40'E-7° 23'E of the Greenwich Meridian. Its spatial extent as indicated by the Federal Office of Statistics is about 5,530 square kilometres. It is bounded on the west and south by Rivers state; on the east by Abia State, and on the north by Anambra State. The area lies on relatively higher terrain averaging 130-200 meters above sea level. The location of Okigwe, Isiala Mbano, and Onuimo is seen in figure.

The 1991 population head count census showed that the total human population of Imo state was 2,485,635 comprising of 1,166,448 males and 1,319,187 females. Okigwe has 97, 229 people comprising 38,009 males and 41, 220 females; Isiala Mbano had 106, 170 people comprising 49, 171 males and 56, 999 females; and Onuimo had 54, 470 comprising 25, 606 males and 28, 864 females (National Population Commission, 2006). The 2006 national population census of the study area is shown in Table 1.

Table 1

2006 National Population Census of the Study Area

Area	Population		Total
	MALES	FEMALES	
Imo State	1,976,471	1,951,092	3,927,563
Okigwe	67,660	65,041	132,701
Isiala Mbano	100,835	97,086	197,921
Onuimo	50,779	48,589	99,368

Source: National Population Commission, Abuja, 2006.

The population of the area is projected to grow at about 2.8% annually. The urban component of the population spreads over headquarters of the three senatorial zones of Owerri, Okigwe, and Orlu in addition to headquarters of the 27 Local Government areas of the State.

Literature Review

Agroforestry is an integrated approach of using the interactive benefits from combining trees and shrubs with crops and/or livestock. It combines agricultural and forestry technologies to create more diverse, productive, profitable, healthy, and sustainable land use systems.

The Food and Agriculture Organization (2018) defines agroforestry as "a collective name for land use systems and technologies where woody perennials (trees, shrubs, palms, bamboos, etc.) are deliberately used in the same land-management units as agricultural crops and or animals in some form of spatial arrangement or temporal sequence." There are normally both ecological and economic interactions between woody and non-woody components in agroforestry. In agroforestry systems, trees or shrubs are intentionally used within agricultural systems, or non-timber forest products are cultured in forest settings. Knowledge, careful selection of species, and good management of trees are needed to optimize the production of positive effect within systems to minimize negative competitive effects (Godsey, 2000). The most common forms of agroforestry practice in Nigeria are taungya system, non-timber tree farms and intercropping of leguminous trees with food crops (Federal Ministry of Environment, 2003).

Merem (2005) notes that prior to the emergence of agroforestry, some ecological zones in Nigeria experienced considerable depletion of their forested areas over the years and this may be attributed to a host of factors associated with anthropogenic activities in the use of land in the country. The problem is evident considering the growing incidence of environmental degradation emanating from sectors of the economy such as agriculture and over dependence on oil revenues. He also notes that the rural nature of the country and their dependence on subsistence farming and ecological ramifications is quickening the gradual spread of agroforestry among Nigerian communities to arrest the problem.

Aweto (2000) reveals that community-based effort in three southern states shows a mix of similarities and divergences in their methods, priorities, and accomplishments. His observation was that farmers in Urhobo area of the Niger Delta practiced integrated farming that uses palm trees alongside other crops to maintain soil fertility. In Ilesha, the Leventis Foundation through a joint venture provided a major boost to education when it backed up its commitment to sustainability by establishing Ilesha agricultural school to educate farmers. One of the major accomplishments involves the design of agroforestry nursery that distinguishes medicinal fruits and wood trees (Slinger, 2001).

In Abia State, several households showed their awareness of positive impact that trees and agroforestry bring to their environment (Odurukwe, 2004). They were involved in community-based efforts to improve soil fertility and reduce erosion as well as enhance food security and household incomes. An analysis of agroforestry practices in southern states offers decision makers the tool to identify the environmental and economic benefits as a road map in the design of viable indices that will guide managers in crafting the appropriate strategies for dealing with the problem (Zing and Dawson, 2004).

Farming activity in Niger Delta region involves both staple food and cash crop production. The major staple food crops include plantain, banana, cocoyam, yam, maize, cassava, vegetable and melon. The major cash crops on the other hand include, oil palm, oranges (*citrus spp.*), kola nut (*cola spp.*), plantain and banana (*musa spp.*), raffia palm (*raffia spp.*), cocoa (*Theobroma cacao*), coconut (*coco nucifera*), and swamp rice (Okpara 2004). He also states that the major natural resources currently being exploited in Nigeria for supposedly meeting the demand for socioeconomic development with the exception of solid, liquid mineral, air and solar power includes agricultural resources of agricultural product such as root crops and cereals; forest products such as timber and non-timber forest products (NTFPs); fishery products and other sea foods; wildlife resources; water resources for agriculture; livestock and land for non-agricultural use (Okpara, 2001).

Oluwasola (1997) states that farmers have been aware of the fragile nature of the rich tropical soils have and in response evolve several agricultural practices to optimally manage the soil resources, improve soil productivity and greater return of their effort. Agricultural practices give way to natural regeneration as farmers allow land to rest for several years. During the period of re-growth, soil nutrients are naturally recycled through the decay of plant litter and residue. However, with the increasing population in the area, the stress on these resources has degraded the soil water and forest.

Azuaga (2008) indicates that the systems and practices of agroforestry in south eastern Benue State have shown that some of practices have been in use for a long while some are adaptations of various systems by farmers. Agroforestry according to him is seen as land use management system that offers solution to land and forest degradation problems. Little effort has been made by both government and non-governmental agencies to introduce modern techniques as found in other parts of the world.

Questionnaire Administration

A structured questionnaire was administered to four hundred and fifty (450) respondents being a representative of the population of the three local government areas under study. One hundred and fifty (150) respondents were sampled from each of the three local government areas using three autonomous communities selected from each of the three local government areas for questionnaire administration. The respondents selected were mostly those that are in agro-based businesses. A randomized quota sampling technique was used to administer the questionnaire to the respondents. 300 respondents representing 68% of the sample were farmers whereas one hundred and fifty respondents (150) representing 23% belonged to other interest groups including traditional rulers, town union presidents and secretaries of various farmers' cooperative unions, staff of the ministries of agriculture and forestry in different local government area headquarters and the state capital. The questionnaire has thirty (24) test items. Information in Table 2 shows questionnaire administration for the study.

Table 2
Questionnaire Distribution

LGA	Community	No. Distributed	Percentage Distributed	No Retrieved	Percentage Retrieved

Okigwe	Ogii	50	11.1	50	11.5
	Isiokwe	50	11.1	49	11.3
	Umulolo	50	11.1	48	11.1
Onu-imo	Umuna	50	11.1	46	10.6
	Umuduru Egbeguru	50	11.1	48	11.1
	Okwelle	50	11.1	47	10.6
Isiala Mbano	Umunkwo	50	11.1	46	10.6
	Amaraku	50	11.1	49	11.3
	Ugiri	50	11.1	50	11.6
Total		450	100	433	96.2

Source: Fieldwork

Presentation And Discussions Of Research Findings

Data collected are presented and analyzed based on the following:
1. Involvement of different cohorts in agroforestry in the study area
2. Occupational and farming/agricultural practices of the respondents
3. Forestry products in the study area
4. Economic benefits/contributions of agroforestry in the area.

Involvement Of Different Cohorts In Agroforestry In The Study Area

Table 3 shows the involvement of different cohorts practicing agroforestry in the study area. The data shows that only 5 of the respondents or 3.5 percent of the total number of respondents sampled are within the age bracket of 16-25 years as against 200 or 46.2% of above 50 years age bracket.

Table 3
Involvement of Different Age Cohorts in Agroforestry in the Study Area

LGA	Community	Cohorts				
		16-25 yrs	26-35 yrs	36-45 yrs	46-55 yrs	> 55
Okigwe	Ogii	0	4	9	8	17
	Isiokwe	3	6	6	20	33
	Umulolo	2	3	4	10	25
Onuimo	Umuna	1	3	5	8	11
	Umuduru Egbeaguru	4	8	6	17	21
	Okwelle	2	2	3	5	8
Isiala Mbano	Umunkwo	1	6	8	17	30
	Amaraku	_	4	7	13	24
	Ugiri	2	15	12	20	31
Total		15	40	60	118	200
% (percentage)		3.5%	9.2%	13.9%	24.3%	46.2%

Source: Field Work

Information from the questionnaire also shows that the occupation of agroforestry in the study area was handled mostly by the ageing men and women (46-55) (24.3%) and above 55 years (46.2%) representing a total of 318 (70.5%) of the sample. It also shows that youths and other members of the active population prefer to engage in fast-yielding ventures such as manufacturing and service industries. It was also gathered that people prefer to engage themselves in the business of agroforestry when they have retired from manufacturing and other service industries and activities. This trend was responsible for food insecurity in the area as agricultural activities are abandoned only to the ageing members of the communities. The observation is also in consonance with the findings of Nwibe (2007) who observed that oil palm production in Oru Local Government Area attracts persons above 55 years of age.

Occupational Distribution Of The Respondents

The occupational distribution of the respondents is presented in Table 4. The table shows that many the respondents from the various communities are self-employed representing about 83 percent of the entire population, while 17 percent are engaged in the public service. Out of the 83 percent in self-employment, 206 or 48 percent are involved in different kinds of farming practice while about 145 representing about 20 percent engage in other agroforestry activities such as timber production and harvesting of palm fruits. About 61 respondents representing about 12 percent of the population are involved in different kinds of trading; fishing is not a major economic activity in the area as the research reveals that only 1.6 percent of the respondents are involved. The results agree with the finding of Onyenechere (2009) who indicates that petty trading and farming are among the major economic activities of the rural women of Imo State, representing 39.7 and 29.1 percent respectively (Onyenechere 2009).

Table 4
Occupational Distribution of the Area

LGA	Com-munity	Occupation						Total
		Civil Service	Farming	Oil Palm Harve	Timber Trade	Trading	Fishing	

					sting			
Okigwe	Ogii	6	26	4	10	4	–	50
	Isiokwe	8	23	3	8	2	5	49
	Umulolo	12	20	2	6	8	–	48
Onu-imo	Umuna	7	18	5	4	10	2	46
	Umudu-ruegbea-guru	4	32	6	3	3	–	48
	Okwelle	10	21	1	4	11	–	47
Isiala Mbano	Umunkwo	6	26	6	5	3	–	46
	Amaraku	12	16	–	7	14	–	49
	Ugiri	10	24	7	3	6	–	50
Total		75	206	34	50	61	7	433
Percentage		17.3	47.6	7.9	11.5	14.1	1.6	

Source: Fieldwork.

Farming And Agricultural Practices Of The Respondents

The data in Table 4 show that the major farming practices obtained in the area are mixed farming and mixed cropping representing 197 (45.5%) and 168 (38.8%) respectively. The two practices together represent about 85 percent of the farming practices of the respondents. Mono cropping is rarely practiced in the area as indicated by 14 respondents representing 3.2 percent. Animal rearing takes 54 or 12.5 percent of the respondents and it is practiced in small scale with greater percentage reared for family consumption and little surplus for sale. The study also gathered that most of these animals are reared in an enclosed area except for poultry animals which are on free range although there are a few large poultry farms in the area where poultry animals are restricted in an enclosed surrounding.

The research also shows that the major reasons for mixed farming and mixed cropping are to minimize cost because labour is less costly and there is dominance of small holdings A good example of mixed farming and mixed cropping observed in the study area is seen in plate one where pineapple orchard and plantain/banana plantations are seen growing together on a piece of land.

Plate 1: Pineapple orchard and plantains/bananas growing together.
Source: Fieldwork.

Examination Of Forest Products In The Study Area

Observation of data obtained from the study indicate that both timber products and non-timber forest products (NTFPs) are produced in the study area. The data on Table 6 show different timber trees indicated by the respondents. The number of major economic trees such as *iroko, mahogany and obeche* has declined drastically as each of them represents 3.5%, 1.2% and 0.0% respectively, totaling about 5% or 20 respondents from the sampled respondents. The data also shows that African oil bean and *gmelina* represent about 71 percent of economic trees in the study. It was however observed that the number of these trees are on the decline because of absence of other economic trees used in building of houses and construction of bridges. The tree most affected because of this trend is *gmelina*. The data on table 4.9 is used to illustrate timber trees indicated by respondents in the study area.

Table 6
Timber Trees in the Study Area

Timber Trees	Number of Respondents	Percentage Score for Each Tree
Iroko	15	3.5
African Oil Bean	225	52
Gmelina	80	18.5
Mahogany	5	1.2
Achi	25	5.8
None	83	19.2
Total	433	100

Source: Fieldwork.

On the method of sale, the respondents as on Table 7 indicates that 338 persons or 78% sold their trees on the farm to timber merchants. 50 respondents representing 11.5% cut their trees into pieces and sell as fuel wood to bakers and other users. 30

respondents or 6.9% convert their tree into charcoal and sell to charcoal dealers.

Table 7
Method of Sale

	Method of Sale	Number of Responses	Percentage
1	Sold live to timber Merchants	338	78.1
2	Processed into timber and sold to Merchants	10	2.3
3	Cuts into pieces and sold as fuel wood	50	11.5
4	Converted into charcoal and sold to dealers	30	6.9
5	Personal use	5	1.2
	Total	433	100.0

Source: Fieldwork.

Socio-Economic Benefits/Contributions Of Agroforestry

Apart from generation of income from NTFPs, socio economic contributions as observed from the study area are highlighted in Table 8. Data on the table shows different socio-economic contributions of agroforestry in the study area. Analysis of the data from the table shows that the major contribution of agro-forestry in the study area is source of food as indicated by 98 respondents or 45.7% of the sample population. Next in rank is that it is a source of employment (59 respondents or 13.6%). This is followed by use for medicinal purpose (48 respondents or 11.1%). Other contributions are reduction in soil erosion

(10.6%); maintenance of soil fertility (10.2%); and source of income (38 respondents or 8.8%).

Table 8
Socio Economic Benefit of Agroforestry

Socio-economic Benefit	Number of Respondents	Percentage
Source of food	198	45.7
Source of income	38	8.8
Medicinal purpose	48	11.1
Source of employment	59	13.6
Maintenance of soil fertility	44	10.2
Control of soil erosion	46	10.6
Total	433	100

Source: Fieldwork.

Non-Timber Forest Products In The Study Area

Different non-timber forest products produced in reasonable quantities are presented in Table 9. *Utazi* and scent leaf rank highest followed by *ukazi* and *uziza.* These are common agroforestry products used in homes in the study area.

Table 9

Local Name	Botanical Name	Number of Respondents	Percentage
Utazi	*Gonronema latifolia*	146	33.7

Ukazi	Gnetum Africana	80	18.5
Scent leaf	Occimum Gratis-simum	100	23.1
Ukpa	Tetracarpidum conophorum	40	9.2
Uziza	Piper guineensis	67	15.5
Total		433	100

Non-Timber Forest Products In The Area

Source: Fieldwork.

The research revealed that above products are mainly produced by women; about 95 percent of non-timber forest products are produced by women. The major motive for production of these NTEPs are for food and income generation.

Summary

The study revealed the following:

1. That agroforestry, though constituting part of the economic activity in the area is not very prominent.
2. The production of non-timber forest products (NTFPs) is undertaken more by women than men while men are more involved in timber production than women.
3. Agroforestry has the potential to reduce the tendency towards slashing and burning of farmlands which cause degradation. This is because the farmers find it unwise to set fire on their slashed farmland that has trees growing on it as this will be very injurious to their NTFPs.
4. Agroforestry in the study area helps to control soil erosion.

Recommendations

To address some of the concerns raised in this study, some recommendations are made which ranges from proper education and research to policy reform. Specifically, the following should be considered:

1. **Encouragement of local involvement in agroforestry:** Authorities should involve local communities in agroforestry programmes by offering assistance that can help develop village tree plantations in woody poor areas dependent on fuel woods for coking and on poles and timber to meet local fencing and building needs.

2. **Promoting Education and Research Efforts:** Research programmes and education to acquaint farmers with the right practices to boost food security and techniques suitable for their respective eco-zones in addressing the problems can help to minimize degradation. The authorities and institutions can also work closely with these communities to develop action plans anchored on local needs in soil management among other needs (Frenzel, 2001).

3. **Providing financial support and right climate for income generation:** The successful implementation of agroforestry programmes as shown by some research requires availability of improved seedlings and planting techniques (Bohringer 2001). Funding to enable farmers secure seedlings and implements would boost crop planting initiatives.

4. Land reform should be made to make for easier and quicker access to land by those prospecting to engage in agroforestry ventures.

Conclusion

This study focused on identifying the role of agroforestry to the socio-economic development of Imo State. Three local government areas namely: Okigwe, Onuimo and Isiala Mbano were used as sample locations for the survey. The study shows that there is not much emphasis on agroforestry in the study area despite the potentials of agroforestry. The study recommends the involvement of government for purposes of education, funding, and research.

References

Aweto, A. (2000). Agriculture in Urhoboland. Paper presented at the 5th Annual Conference of Urhobo Historical Society at Petroleum Training Institute Conference Centre, Effurum, Delta State.

Azuaga, K.T. (2008). Agroforestry and land management for agricultural intensification. In F. E. Bisong, *Geography and millennium development goals, Translating vision into reality.* Association of Nigerian Geographers Book of Proceedings. Calabar: Index Book Publishers Limited

Bisong, F.E. (2007). Land use and deforestation in south-eastern Nigeria (1972-2001). *Nigerian Geographical Journal.* 5 (1).

Bohringer, A. (2001). Facilitating the wide use of agroforestry for development in Southern Africa. *Development in practice.* 11. 434-448.

Central Intelligence Agency (2000). World fact book. Retrieved, 1st December 2017 from   www.odci.gov.cia

Food and Agriculture Organization (FAO). (2001). Global forest paper 140. Rome: UNFAO.

Federal Ministry of Environment (FME). (2003). *National convention on climate change.* Abuja: Federal Ministry of Environment.

Food and Agriculture Organization (2018). Agroforestry. Retrieved, 2nd January 2018 from http://www.fao/forestry/agroforestry/80338/en

Franzel, S. P. C., & Denning, G. L. (2007). Scaling up the benefits of agroforestry research: Lessons learned and research challenges. *Development in practice.* 11. 4.

Godsey, L. D. (2000). *Economic budgeting for agroforestry practices.* Columbia: University of Missouri.

Mantu, I. (2003). Implications of population growth for the Nigerian economy and development. Abuja: Olive de Afrique Consult.

Mende, M. (2003). Agroforestry: A tool for accelerated socio-economic improvement of rural livelihood in Nigeria. Department of Forest Resource Management, Faculty of Agriculture and Forestry, University of Ibadan.

Merem, E. (2005). The agroforestry systems of West Africa: A case study of Nigeria. AFFTA Conference Proceedings.

National Academy of Sciences (1982). Ecological aspects of development in the humid tropics. Washington, D.C.

Odurukwe, S. (2004). Agroforestry in peri-urban cities of Abia State, Nigeria. U.M.M. 8-9.

Okpara, E. E. (2001). Managing natural resources in Nigeria. Paper presented at the Nigerian Academy of Sciences Quarterly Forum, Umuahia, Abia State.

Okpara, E. E (2004). *Post-Rio realities of sustainable development in the Niger Delta region of Nigeria.* Owerri: Ihem Davis Press Limited.

Oluwasola, O. (1997). Agroforestry for sustainable rural development in Benue State. Paper presented on 1997 World Environment Day, 5th June 1997. BSEPA Makurdi.

Onyenechere, E.C. (2009). Effect of rural women informal economic activities on employment creation in Imo State. *The Nigerian Geographic Journal.* 5 (22).

Salau, A.T. (1993). Environmental crises and development in Nigeria. Inaugural Lecture Series No. 13, University of Port Harcourt, Nigeria.

nadeo2k6@yahoo.com
osumgborogwu.ikenna@gmail.com
jamesnnamdi86@gmail.com

CHAPTER 5

ENTREPRENEURIAL OPPOR-
TUNITIES IN THEATRE PRAXIS
AND THE ENTERTAINMENT
INDUSTRY IN NIGERIA

Ime G. MORISON
Department of Theatre Arts
Federal College of Education (Technical)
Omoku, Nigeria

Abstract

The uniqueness of theatre practice is such that it is geared towards the creation, packaging, presentation and dissemination of cultural entertainments to groups of people gathered to share in the experience. The public nature of its presentation, consumption and appreciation is, notably, one of the reasons theatrical entertainments is often referred to as 'show business'. Though theatre practice or show business, as with other businesses, maybe capital intensive and unprofitable if not well managed; however, the collaborative nature of theatre practice makes it such that networks of viable entrepreneurial opportunities are easily created and harnessed by theatre graduates in terms of business start-ups, job creation and wealth generation. Drawing from the descriptive research methodology, this paper shall attempt an in-depth examination of the opportunities embedded in the world theatre practice and the entertainment industry. The paper shall, therefore, recommend a robust investment, management and support of entrepreneurs in the cultural and creative sector as one of the strategies that could help tackle unemployment, create wealth as well as pull the country out of the current economic recession.

Keywords: Entrepreneurship, Opportunities, Theatre Praxis, Entertainment Industry.

Introduction

Until recently, young adults in the country, who expressed interests in studying or pursuing a career in the arts of the theatre and the entertainment industry, were faced with stiff opposition from parents and guardians who perceived that only professional courses like law, medicine, engineering, accounting were worth studying or practicing. As such, theatre practitioners as well as those in the cultural and creative industry were considered academic failures and those who would never do well in life (Osofisan, 2005; Johnson, 2013). This is because these professions, especially the performing arts of theatre, music and dance, was considered, at the time, only fit for vagabonds or people of loose morals; and most parents could not process why agile youths would want to spend years in school only to learn how to sing, drum and dance or people, in the larger society, who would likely pay to watch such commonplace cultural performances or entertainments (Ayakoroma, 2012; Osofisan, 2005). However, the emergence of the Nigerian movie industry (Nollywood), its commercial success, popularity as well as the successes of artistes in other areas of the entertainment industry and show business, most notably, music and stand-up comedy have played significant roles in altering certain hard-lined perceptions about the economic viability of the theatre profession, show business and the entertainment industry in general.

Now, the tides have changed and the boom in the performance, cultural and creative industry in the country is such that many professionals have abandoned their degrees in fields such as law, engineering, medicine and accounting to venture into opportunities available in theatre practice and the entertainment industry. While most are attracted to the glamour and fame of television and film acting, others are focused on exploring the entrepreneurial opportunities existing in the industry to create wealth via innovation and creative thinking. As entrepreneurship studies have, in recent times, directed its focus not just on the identification but also the utilization or transformation of identified opportunities into business start-ups, job creation and wealth generation; this paper shall leverage on extant entrepreneurial models as its theoretical frame, to examine the viability of opportunities in theatre praxis and the entertainment industry in Nigeria. Before advancing into this examination, as it were, certain background issues such a discourse on the nature of theatre praxis and the world of show business as well as a cursory overview of theatre as an academic discipline shall be, fore mostly, attempted.

Theoretical Framework

It is often asserted that theories are the primary means of identifying, defining, prescribing or evaluating an applied problem as well as providing speculative answers or functioning as a means of responding to perceived or new problems that have no previously identified solutions (Walliman, 2011; Ardichvili, Cardozo and Ray, 2003). Entrepreneurship literature has, in recent years, projected the ability of identifying and selecting right opportunities for businesses as among the most important abilities of a successful entrepreneur (Stevenson et al, 1985; Ardichvili et al, 2003). Various researches have been carried out, in this regard, in view of explaining the discovery and development of entrepreneurial opportunities (Venkataraman, 1997). Consequently, numerous models have been presented (Sigirst, 1999; De Koning, 1999; Bhave, 1994); however, the theoretical framework for this paper shall be hinged on Ardichvili et al (2003) theory of entrepreneurial opportunity identification and development. This is because a review of this theory shall, fundamentally, aid the understanding and thrust of the subject-matter in this paper.

Notably, the process of opportunity identification and development is highly complex and draws analysis from a broad spectrum of disciplines such as management, marketing, organisation theory and entrepreneurship (Ardichvili et al, 2003). Drawing from this rich multi-disciplinary foundation, and particularly from Dubin's (1978) methodology for theory building, Ardichvili et al (2003) have proposed a theory of entrepreneurial opportunity identification and development which captures a model and units for the creation of a successful business from a successful opportunity development process. This process includes "recognition of an opportunity, its evaluation and development" (Ardichvili et al, 2003:118). As a development process, Ardichvili et al (2003:118), assert that it is cyclical and iterative because "an entrepreneur is likely to conduct evaluation several times at different stages of development, and these evaluations could lead to recognition of additional opportunities or to adjustments to the initial vision". In view of this, Ardichvili et al (2003) aver that:

> The core process in the model begins when the entrepreneur has an above-threshold level of entrepreneurial alertness. This level of entrepreneurial alertness is likely to be heightened when there is a coincidence of several factors: certain personality traits like creativity and optimism are critical determinants of this alertness; as are the domains of knowledge: Domain 1 (special interest) and Domain 2 (knowledge and experience in a specific product and customer market). The nature of social networks (including

weak ties, action set, partnerships and inner circle) also
determines the level of this entrepreneurial alertness. Finally, the type of opportunity plays an important role in
shaping this core process (p. 118).

From the above, Ardichvili et al (2003) have formulated the
following propositions to illustrate the theory of opportunity
identification:

Proposition 1: A high level of entrepreneurial alertness is
associated with successful opportunity recognition and development.

Proposition 2: Successful opportunity identification is associated with the existence and use of extended social network,
which includes the following four elements: weak ties, action
set, partnerships, and inner circle. The lack of any of any of these
elements reduces the probability of such success.

Proposition 3: For successful opportunity identification, a
convergence of both the knowledge domains – special interest
knowledge and industry knowledge – is critical. Without this
convergence there is a lower probability of success.

Proposition 4: Prior knowledge of markets increases the likelihood of successful entrepreneurial opportunity recognition.

Proposition 5: Prior knowledge of customer problems increases the likelihood of successful entrepreneurial opportunity
recognition.

Proposition 6: Prior knowledge of ways to serve markets increases the likelihood of successful entrepreneurial opportunity
recognition.

Proposition 7: High levels of entrepreneurial alertness are
related to high levels of entrepreneurial creativity and optimism
(based on high self-efficacy).

Proposition 8: The opportunity identification process results in
enriching the entrepreneur's knowledge base and increase in
alertness, leading to the identification of future business opportunities. Thus, the greater the number of previously successful
opportunity identification events, the higher the probability of
future successful identification events.

Although Ardichvili et al (2003) theory of entrepreneurial opportunity identification conceives opportunity identification/recognition as a multi-staged process which entrepreneurs play proactive roles based on influence from individual and situational difference; and ultimately, require extensive validation from future research and application, it, however, provides a useful starting point for this paper's examination of entrepreneurial opportunities in the theatre and entertainment industry in Nigeria.

The Nature Of Theatre Praxis And Show Business

A conceptual appraisal of the term theatre shows that it could be defined or understood from a plethora of perspectives and the multiplicity of meanings entails that the term could denotatively mean different things to many people. For instance, as defined in the Cambridge Advance Learners Dictionary and Thesaurus (online), the term holds a divergent meaning in a wide-ranging field of knowledge such as architecture, medicine, performing arts, education, military and behavioural studies. Nevertheless, Ayakoroma (2012) contends that these perspectives of meanings offer significant insights, as it were, to the understanding and functioning of theatre as a creativity-laden and technique-based practice.

Drawing from its etymology in Greek 'theatron', the theatre is often conceived as a 'place of seeing' (Ayakoroma, 2012; Betiang, 2001) or "an arena or building for dramatic performance or other Thespian arts" (Betiang, 2001:13).Burns (1973:5) describes the theatre as "an arena in which it is possible to study manifestations of the social values, forms and conventions of society and also the images of social reality which different people have construed for themselves". According to Ayakoroma (2012: n. p.), the theatre is that "art, which the public viewed, and still view today, as a basic nature of man's means of expressing his internal perception of life". From these defining standpoints, it is glaring that the theatre, as an art form, places imagined human experiences before a group of people – an audience or perceivers – who gather to share in its experience (Barranger, 1984; Wilson, 2004). The nature of its existence or creation process is hinged, fundamentally, on the interaction of three basic or essential elements: what is performed (script, scenario or plan, dance, music etc.); the performance (including all the processes involved in the creation and presentation of a production); and the audience - the perceivers (Brockett and Ball, 2004; Langley, 1981; Wilson, 2004; Ayakoroma, 2012). The processes involved in the creation and exhibition of theatrical entertainments underscore its nature as a complex and collaborative art (Nwamuo, 2003; Ohiri, 2005; Inyang, 2016). This is so because theatre is a team effort that requires the collaboration of many creatively-skilled artists, workers and then spectators in its conception and eventual delivery (Barranger, 1984). Thus, within this collaborative ambience, creatively-skilled artists such as the playwright, director, designers (light, scene, costume and make-up, sound, props etc.) and actors come together to create the total theatre event by transforming an empty stage into an environment where actors live out special moments of their make-believe lives in their make-believe world; for the audience, who becomes a part and parcel of the collaboration by watching each performance and responding to the success or failure of this collective enterprise (Barranger, 1984; Achoakawa, 2015).

The implication of this is that the audience, spectators or perceivers play a central, integral or prominent role in the existence of the theatre and the entertainment industry both as an art form and as a business enterprise. The reason for this is not far-fetched as there can be no show or theatrical event without the people who have gathered to 'see' and enjoy the experience 'shown'; hence, the reference "show business". It has been noted variously that the theatre and entertainment business cannot thrive without the audience (Nwamuo, 2014; Nwamuo, 2003; Ohiri, 2005; Awodiya, 2006). As a serious business whose underlying aim is the generation of enough box office to cover cost, pay and sustain the actors or showman as well as make profits (Ekweariri, 2014; Essien and Oqua, 2008), patronage by audience member is critically fundamental in theatre praxis and the entertainment business (Apeh, 2011). This is because theatrical productions or cultural entertainments are "conceived, rehearsed, packaged and presented for audience members whose continual patronage assures the survival of the theatre" (Ekweariri, 2014: 96). Thus, it could be asserted that the theatre and entertainment industry is predominantly saddled with the responsibility of producing artistic goods and services which are marketed to the audience to elicit patronage (Ekweariri, 2014).

Although the very idea of business in theatre praxis could revile most economist who hold the view that a product of market value must be concrete, tangible and needs-motivated, Fosudo (2014) contends that theatre is a service-product which begins as an idea that can be packaged or transformed into valuable services to be offered or provided to satisfy the needs of a segment of the consuming public. Fosudo's (2014) position aligns with Hill et al's (1998) assertion that the business activity of a theatre could be viewed in terms of physical productions, which could be referred to as "central experience", or additional or auxiliary services which may include rental of space and other company equipment such as sound system, light, audio and video recordings as well as catering; which could be described, jointly, as "extended experience". It, therefore, follows that theatre and entertainment by its nature as art form and business, shares the characteristics of intangibility, inseparability, variability, lack of ownership, high customer contact and perishability with service-based sectors such as tourism and transportation (Fosudo, 2014; Cannon, 1994; Pride and Ferrel, 1995; Evans and Berman, 1992). As such, it is in this vein that Nwamuo (2014:19) submit that theatre and cultural entertainments must be "well-fashioned (i.e. of good quality), well-packaged, advertised and delivered or presented to the satisfaction of the audience". Hence, venturing into the business of theatre and cultural entertainment demands sound entrepreneurial skills, management acumen and strategies to identify, recognize, and develop opportunities embedded in the theatre and allied creative cum cultural entertainment industry.

Theatre As An Academic Discipline

Theatre, as an academic discipline and practice is traceable to the classical ages of Ancient Greece and Rome (Idogho, 2013). Theatre Arts is a discipline that teaches all the arts necessary for the creation, packaging and dissemination of cultural performances or entertainments. It brings together elements and personnel such as performers (actors, dancers, comedians, jugglers, and others), playwright, director, designers (light, scene, sound, costume and make-up), critics, managers, and administrators into a collaboration for the goal of creating an aesthetically viable experience for the audience or perceivers (Brocket and Ball, 2004; Wilson, 2004).

Whilst the emergence of theatre as a commercial practice in Nigeria is traced to the pioneering efforts of Hubert Ogunde and other Yoruba travelling theatre practitioners such as Duro Ladipo, Kola Ogumola, Ade Afolayan, Baba Salah etc. in the 1940s (Ogunbiyi, 1981; Ogundeji, 2016); theatre as an academic discipline in Nigeria emerged in the 1960s when the University of Ibadan through funds made available by the Rockefeller Foundation and help from expatriates like Martin Banham, Geoffrey Axworthy and Dexter Lindersay offered arts diploma courses to non-graduates and graduates in the 1963/64 session via its School of Drama (Idogho, 2013). The School of Drama at the University of Ibadan later metamorphosed into a full-fledge theatre department and led to the establishment of theatre departments elsewhere, most notably, at the University of Nigeria, Nsukka and the University of Calabar, Calabar respectively. Since then the growth of the theatre as an academic discipline has been rapid such that over 50% of Universities and Colleges of Education in Nigeria now operate an educational theatre programme, though with different appellation such as Creative Arts, Performing Arts, Drama, Theatre, Film or Media Arts respectively.

It is germane to note that the attraction to theatre studies seem to stem from the fact that it provides or exposes its students to a well-rounded education in the arts and praxis of cultural and contemporary entertainments. A cursory assessment of the discipline's curriculum show that theatre studies synthesizes theory and practice as well as offer specialization in different but related arts such as dramatic literature, theory and criticism; history and sociology of drama; theatre in education, children's theatre or creative dramatics; community theatre, theatre for development or applied theatre, the media (radio, television and film/video, writing and broadcasting); music production and sound effects, make-up, costume design and construction, set design and construction; lighting design and appliances, advertising and public relation, publicity and theatre business management, stage and studio management; dance and choreography; acting, mime and movement; directing (for stage, tv/film and radio), props design and construction amongst others.

Entrepreneurial Opportunities In Theatre Praxis And Entertainment Industry

As a field of study geared towards the discovery, evaluation and exploitation of opportunities independently (Darren and Conrad, 2009), entrepreneurship has emerged recently as the most dominant economic force by revolutionizing and changing the manner in which businesses are established and conducted (Lucky, 2014). Entrepreneurship development is, increasingly, acknowledged as an essential instrument for achieving economic growth and transformation, wealth creation, employment generation and talent development across global economies (Rebecca and Benjamin, 2009; Lucky, 2014). Nevertheless, the task of identifying or recognizing opportunities in the environment, mobilizing resources to take advantage of available opportunities to provide goods and services for customers and maximize profits therefrom (Ogundele, 2007); is not an easy one as one must critically consider the risks involved in the venture as well as the viability of opportunities available in the industry, amongst other things. In this instance, therefore, the theatre, entertainment or cultural and creative arts industry has been identified as having the potential to diversify the economy as well as facilitate cultural, socio-economic development of developing countries such as Nigeria (Idiahi, 2011). However, due to a multiplicity of issues such as governmental neglect, lack of foresight and attention from entrepreneurs and investors as well as paucity of funds or investment capital, the opportunities embedded in this sector in Nigeria has remained, largely, unidentified and unexplored.

A critical examination of the theatre arts discipline, as earlier noted, shows the existence of networks of viable entrepreneurial opportunities that theatre graduates and other entrepreneurs could explore through targeted innovation and strategic investment. These opportunities would be exhumed and briefly discussed from the various areas of specialization found in theatre practice, namely; dance and choreography, costume and make-up, artists and events management, stand-up comedy, syndicated scripting and content development, scene/ lighting design, videography and filmography, children's theatre, creative dramatics and theatre-in-education, community theatre and theatre-for-development, and so on.

Dance And Choreography

Dance is one of the major performative art form in theatre praxis and a valuable cultural entertainment. It has been described variously as: the rhythmic movement of the body in time and space to communicate or express an idea emotion or feeling (Obongko and Onwuka, 2016; Ojo, 2004) a universal non-verbal language through which culture is expressed, interpreted, transmitted and nurtured (Tume, 2014) or a patterned and rhythmic bodily movements, visually performed to music that serve as a form of communication or expression (Funk and Wagnalls, 1971). The import of these definition is that dance, as an art form, is a veritable medium through which information, messages, ideas and entertainment are communicated or projected or expressed through the dancer's body to onlookers or audience (Oluwafemi, 2016). In this view, dance serves as a language that expresses "the geographical locations, biological temperature, religion beliefs, political and historical experiences, social practices and economic peculiarities of the people that own it" (Ojo, 2004).

As a cultural phenomenon, dance is common place in every culture and is of a multi-functional value in the African milieu (Tume,2016). This is because the functionality of the medium transcends religious, social, ritualistic and existential realms. Thus, Tume (2016) highlight that:

> Dance is used for worship, to appease supernatural/ supreme powers, to aspire for a better life; rains; good harvest, to encourage warriors on their way to the battle-front, to welcome and celebrate good news, rites of passage; naming, initiations, wedding and burial ceremonies (p. 32).

Within these contexts of performance, dance elements such as movements, space or floor, body patterns, music, instrument, and others are purposefully arranged to reflect the message inherent in the dance. This is usually done by a dance artist or choreographer whose specialty is the designing of dance movements and sequences to specify motion and form. Thus, choreography is the business of arranging and designing dance movements for artistic communication and entertainment (Lucky, 2014).

From an entrepreneurial perspective, the business potentials in dance and choreography is both exciting and lucrative. This is because contemporary dance and choreography have broadened in scope to such an extent that it has become a fixture in most local and international religious or secular events. For instance, dance and choreography is an integral part of feature films, music videos, cheerleading, gymnastics, fashion shows, ice skating, marching band, synchronized swimming etc. It is also utilized during the opening and closing ceremonies of major sporting events such as Olympic Games, Commonwealth Games, World Cups, Competition finals, games festivals, carnivals and so on. In the local environment, as highlighted by Tume (2016) dance and choreography, both cultural and contemporary break-dancing styles, are featured in traditional marriages, wedding ceremonies, burial ceremonies, child naming and dedication ceremonies, political rallies or campaigns, street adverts/products promotion etc. Investors or theatre graduates who are alert to these opportunities could organize themselves into groups of performing troupes, conceive or package quality dance productions to meet the demands of these events in their immediate environment.

Community Theatre And Theatre For Development

Community theatre or theatre for development is a form of theatre that has drama and theatre not only as media for entertainment, education and research, but also for information and development of conscientisation of communities about their socio-political situation in order to bring about change (Andrew Essien and Orim 2014; Inyang and Morison, 2016). It is a theatre that is directed towards meeting the developmental needs to the people and community (Inyang, 2015). As a theatre founded on the principles, belief, and understanding that the idea or power of change or development reside with the people, Community theatre or theatre for development is participatory in nature i.e. it allows everybody in the community to take part in all aspects of performance and discourse geared towards engendering change within the community (Inyang and Morison, 2016; Andrew-Essien and Orim, 2014). Based in this, community theatre has been acknowledged as a veritable instrument for addressing societal concerns and needs as well as development issues such as illiteracy, environmental degradation, sanitation, hygiene, epidemic prevention and disease control amongst rural population (Inyang and Morison, 2016; Achoakawa, 2014). This is normally done through change communication, advocacy and sensitisation using indigenous knowledge systems or traditional crudes of communication as fundamental elements of the performance created and enacted by community people. Emerging in the 1970s via Paulo Freire's development theories and Augusto Boal's praxis, community theatre or theatre for development is frequently described as democratic theatre, that is, theatre for the people, by the people, about the people and from the people (Ogu-Rapheal, 2009; Achoakawa, 2014). Its process or methodology is summarised by Breed (2002) thus:

1. Practitioners live within the community or may visit the community on an on-going bases for a long duration of time (the emphasis at this stage is to adjust to the cultural norms, build trust/ relationship and observe daily life);

2. Community members create performance based on issues related to the cause of their underdevelopment;

3. Key issues are researched and linked by practitioners to non- governmental organizations and government organization which may have relations to the cause solution to the issues;

4. Solutions are created through participatory theatre in which the community act out interventions;

5. Action plans are created for community, governmental and international applications (p.1).

Over time, this process of engendering consciousness and development among community people has proved useful, in this regard, to such an extent that numerous non-governmental organization (NGOs) and governmental organization (GOs), both international and national, have resorted to its utilization as a major platform in their development initiative (Inyang and Morison, 2016). In view of this, avid entrepreneurs could position themselves as consultants and partners to the various NGOs, GOs and international organizations such as United States Agency for International Development (USAID), United Nations, United Nations Educational, Scientific, and Cultural Organization (UNESCO), World Health Organization (WHO), Food and Agricultural Organization (FAO), United Nations Children Fund (UNICEF) in the conception, planning or providing logistics, distribution and delivery of these developmental aids or programmes to rural communities.

Theatre/ Drama In Education And Creative Dramatics

The potentials of drama and theatre in the communication of ideas, concepts and thought-provoking messages to audience or learners through spontaneity and make-believe is undeniable (Postin-Anderson, 2008). This is because drama and theatre does not only retell stories in action but presents its audiences with real-life situation and challenges they may have encountered or could encounter and offer profound insights to how these could be addressed or surmounted. Hence, drama and theatre serve as a platform for education and have, over the years, been utilized as a teaching and learning method or techniques in formal education. Drama and theatre-in-education are the approaches and techniques which uses theatre and drama as a teaching and learning medium (Wessels, 1987).

Apart from using drama and theatre to impart knowledge in an educational institution, drama and theatre-in-education makes use of participatory methods of teaching rather than traditional methods which only places emphasis on the teacher an embodiment of knowledge. Learning and teaching through drama and theatre is contextual i.e. it focuses on particulars at the concrete level rather than abstractions (Bolton, 1998; Idogho, 2016). For instance, instead of teaching students' concepts such as freedom, bondage or slavery by defining these words first, the teacher could facilitate or create a process whereby students first experience the idea or concept of slavery or freedom within an imagined dramatic or theatrical situation. Thus, the impact of such experiential learning is such that the students may never forget. As it employs the use of imagination, stimulates creative ability and spirit of inquisitiveness, the use of drama and theatre-in-education can lead to the development of broader understanding through "generalising and making connections" via the personal involvement that initially engages and motivates students in their learning process (Fleming, 1995; Idogho, 2016:5).

Another drama-based technique or method of teaching and learning closely related to drama and theatre-in-education is creative dramatics. The term, also known variously as process drama, child drama, play making, child play, role drama, educational drama etc. (Anjorin, 2016); is "an improvisational, process-centred, non-exhibitional form of drama in which participants are guided by a leader to imagine, act and reflect upon the human experience" (Wagner, 1998). Here, creative dramatics leverages on the direction of the teacher-facilitator in harnessing participant's impulse to play in the improvisation of action and dialogue to give form and meaning to the experience. Although not primarily concerned with teaching theatre skills, even though this may occur along the process, creative drama or dramatics is particularly aimed at developing the skills or imagination, spontaneity, vivid embodiment, mental flexibility by utilizing the natural dramatic impulse in participants to facilitate learning in an unlimited number of fields or areas (Anjorin, 2016). This is done through various means such as role play, storytelling, puppetry, dance, music, games, mime, and pictures. According to Offoboche (1998) the creative drama process entails that the leader or teacher or facilitator provides the participants with the stimuli upon which the drama is built on. It provides the starting point and problems, for which the participants find solutions and the participants invent on the spot story-lines, characters, dialogue and action.

In view of the above, a look at the educational system from pre-primary to tertiary in this country, shows that there is a profound need for teachers or educators, who could inspire, motivate and creatively nurture learners to academic excellence through participatory teaching and learning processes. Hence, an enterprising theatre graduate could tap into this opportunity either through independent practice as teacher-facilitator or children's theatre instructor to various educational institutions within his/her locale or setup a consultancy service whereby workshops, seminars, symposium etc. are carried out or organized to train teachers on these participatory, drama and theatre-based techniques of teaching and learning.

Scriptwriting and Content Development

Scriptwriting or playwriting is generally seen as the creative process of creating or developing dramatic contents for the stage, television, film and recently, video games. It is the art and craft of developing stories with cultural contents based on happenings in the society through dialogue, characters, form, themes, and setting in order to showcase an experience (Nwazue, 2016; James, 2016). Scripting is a highly creative, meticulous and challenging art of the theatre (Fasoranti, 2011) as the playwright or scenarist attempts to create form out of the mass of disordered existence, happenings, situations and experiences. Rea and Irving (2001) assert that dramatic content is created or developed via a "cultural idea" initiated by the playwright through the presentation of both external and internal ideas in the script. According to them, the external ideas are societal ideas or issues which stems from what is seen from his immediate environment while internal ideas are ideas that evolve from the creative imagination of the playwright (Rea and Irving, 2001:12). As such, in the process of developing content, the playwright selects characters, build stories and put ideas into work. He does this by employing his artistic gift or creative vision of seeing into life and fortifying pieces of art with meaningful insights (Smiley, 1971:4). As noted by Smiley (1971), a writer's vision consists of a graphic system or emotional and intellectual perceptions, sentiments, and beliefs. Thus, the playwright is not just a social observer, commentator, critic but also an interpreter of all socio-political phenomena in his milieu (James, 2016). He creates an artistic work out of materials in his environment or society, garnishes it with diverse thematic inspirations which are presented and interpreted in diverse artistic forms.

The business of scriptwriting entails the generation of dramatic contents for stage, radio, computer/video games, film/movies, television and multimedia productions. Emerging trends in the entertainment industry, especially television, radio, computer games and film productions, is that content development for these media has become increasingly syndicated i.e. created or produced, packaged and delivered to many media companies. The popularity of seasonal films has led to the emergence of script conferencing, where many scriptwriters come together to contribute ideas towards developing and writing different episodes of the same film. The nature of the business is such that theatre graduate or entrepreneurs could write scripts or develop content for different media production companies or s/he could establish a company employing writers who create content, package and deliver these scripts on demand.

Costume And Make-Up

Costume and make-up are design sub-set in theatre praxis and entertainment industry. They play important roles as interpretative tools in communicating salient information about characters in theatre, and film and other entertainment performances. Costumes are considered the most intimate aspect of the visual theatre experience because the characters wear them (Akpan, 2013; Bade-Afuye, 2015). According to Utoh-Ezeajugh (2009:130), costumes are "the items of clothing, accessories and ornaments worn by the actor or actress for the purpose of defining characters and establishing the circumstances of the character's existence by situating him/her in time and place" (p.130). Costumes includes all the accessories the performer carries as part of his character as well as all the items related to his hair, dressing, and everything associated with his face, body, make-up including mask, if they are substitute for facial make-up (Bade-Afuye, 2015). Costumes are designed to reveal details about the character's occupation, wealth, mood, status, race, religion, gender and political traits (Akpan, 2013; Bade-Afuye, 2015).

Make-up, on the other hand, is the process of changing the external features of peoples' appearances to give an appealing look. It is the art of rearranging the external appearance of a performer, primarily; his/her face, with the aid of paints, plastics, hair patches, wigs and different hair-dos to depict a type of character desired by the director for the effective communication of the message or meanings embedded in the production. In relation with costume, make up is an aspect of theatre design geared towards creating or recreating a definitive character and appearance as imagined by the playwright and as envisioned by the director towards effective stage communication. It helps to establish the age, state of health and race of an actor (Brocket and Ball, 2004) and may also suggest profession, basic attitudes and self-regard. It aids expressiveness when emphasises is placed on facial features to make them more visible for the audience (Bade-Afuye, 2015).

The entrepreneurial opportunity in costume and make-up business is enormous. A theatre graduate or investor, with fashion design skills, can create costumes for stage, television and film productions as well as for other performing artistes such as dancers, comedians, television broadcasters and musicians. A make-up artist can do same for productions across these media and could as well serve as stylist for the listed performing artistes. Also, the emergence and popularity of bridal make-overs has created another viable market for costume and make-up designers. Thus, an enterprising investor could set-up and mange a costume studio or boutique where bridal accessories are designed or created, sold and distributed or a make-up studio for the distribution of make-up kits, equipment and accessories.

Solo Performance And Stand-Up Comedy

Solo performance could be described simply as the performance a done by one person alone without a companion or the aid of another before an audience (Nnachi, 2014; Agoma, 2016). This type of theatre praxis emerged in the mild 20th century and has the convention of presentation in which "the single actor or actress by means of a prepared and rehearsed text, or via an improvised scenario, as an assumed character or in his or her own person, helps and sustain the interest and attention of an audience for an evening" (Cairney, 2001, p.1). What this implies is that solo performances could be done with or without scripts as a play where one person talks directly to others, with nothing or no one getting between them. (Catron, 2000). According to Catron (2000) the uniqueness of solo production is that:

> It illustrates the power of one – a solitary performer pre-senting a theatrical experience as richly vibrant and varied as multi-character plays...; it may bring to life a historical or fictional character or even an autobiographical story. It may be a drama or comedy; and it may be a story of one per-son or it may involve several other characters that the actor evokes in the audience's imagination – but there is only one actor (pp 1-2).

Thus, not only does Catron's (2000) explication above capture the fact that solo performances are very special performances by very talented individuals (Agoma, 2011), it also establishes stand-up comedy as an aspect of solo performance.

Over the last decade or there about, stand-up comedy has become a popular form of mass entertainment in Nigeria. This variant of solo performance is mostly associated with humorous performances or discourse intended to amuse people (Lucky, 2014). The stand-up comedy business in Nigeria has grown exponentially and is now very lucrative with established performers such as Alibaba, Julius Agu, Gbenga Adeyinka, Okey Bakassi, Yibo Koko and many others setting the pace for up-coming stand-up comedians. The successes of the have attracted many entrepreneurs or investors into the art as some estimates the amount of money comedians charge per show today surpasses the annual income of a regular banker (Agoma, 2016). Thus, theatre graduates or entrepreneurs could explore opportunities in this sector of solo performance by utilizing their talents, skills and training in the arts of acting, public speaking, content development, marketing and branding to excel in this regard.

Scenography And Lighting Design

Designing for the theatre or theatre design is a broad specialty area in theatre praxis that is geared towards a creative and interpretative understanding of a play's meaning via visual recreations. Theatre designers create meanings through concrete images, visual and aural forms to help the audience understand the production better (Okeke, 2016). According to Gillete (2000), the artistes who perform this role includes the set, light, costume, make-up, props and sound designers. They are collectively known as scenographers and their art is called scenography. Thus, scenography involves situating a performance within "a specific and identifiable environment as well as the delineation of characters as it concerns costumes, its attendant accessories and properties and the proper illumination of the performance to enhance the audience's appreciation of the said performance" (Okeke, 2016, p. 113). This practice demands amongst other things adequate knowledge of the principles and elements of design as well as fair knowledge of graphics and the rudiments of carpentry, fine and applied arts, tailoring, and electrical engineering as well as a mastery of architectural principles (Okeke, 2016). Thus, scenographic practice is an integral part of theatrical productions since it gives the performance form and situates it within a culturally acceptable domain (Okeke, 2016).

In view of this, the business of designing of scenic backgrounds and lighting is a major scenographic practice in the theatre, film and entertainment industry. Though this enterprise may be considered capital intensive by theatre entrepreneurs, especially lighting design as it is steeped in technology-driven equipment, exciting and lucrative opportunities abound. For instance, not many professional theatre lighting companies exist in the country and those in existence are majorly regionalised with Duru Oni's DSV Limited, Wase Kaseem's Zmirage Multimedia, Theo Lawson's Goldmine, Alphonsus Orisaremi's Theatre Project Limited, Biodun Abe's Kaaba Production, Ayo Allah Dare's Twilight Media and Molinta Enendu's Molinta Enendu and Company. Therefore, an enterprising theatre graduate could kickstart his or her career in professional scenography practice by providing lighting services to local church shows such as crusades and praise concerts; school or community pageants and talent shows etc, and gradually expand the enterprise by acquiring equipment from incomes generated.

Theatre, Artists And Events Management

Management has evolved over the years into one of the most widely-applied multi-disciplinary concept and knowledge (Idung, 2016). Management has been described as the body of knowledge about managing (Light, 1982). Managing is regarded as the process of planning, organising, directing, coordinating and controlling men, materials, machines and money to secure the optimum achievement of objectives (Light, 1982). Drawing from this, Yalokwu (2002) defines management as the process of planning, organising, leading and controlling the efforts of organizational members and using all other organizational resources of achieve set goals. Therefore, to manage, according to

Lucey (1987) is to plan for something to take place; to make and issue decision to execute the plan; to monitor the results of the executed plan to control events by making them conform to the plan or, if necessary, by modifying the plan.

From the foundational concepts as explained above, theatre management has been variously defined contextually to mean the planning, organising, motivating, directing, staffing and controlling the affairs of the theatre to actualize the goals of achieving a good production, having a full house and maximising profit (Frimpong, 2013; Nwamuo, 2003; Ohiri, 1999). Management in the theatre and entertainment industry covers the process of theatrical performances from script selection or content development to end of production and emphasises aspects such as artist's management, production management, stage and house management, front of house operations, marketing and audience engineering as well as auxiliary services such as catering and events management. While artist management involves the planning or co-ordination of the career as well as the effective representation and welfare, of the artist; events management borders on the conception, organization, packaging and successful delivery of entertainment events. The onerous task and time-consuming nature of these activities have made it such that corporate bodies, organizations and individuals have increasingly enlisted the help of services enterprise in the handling of these events.

The business opportunities in theatrical and entertainment management are enormous. For instance, apart from a small fraction of artistes in the music industry, most Nollywood performers have no agents or managers to coordinate their schedules or represent, market and protect their image rights and brands to the public; negotiate deals or source for endorsements on their behalf. All these things are done, mostly, by the artist themselves. Furthermore, talent agencies that could identify, grow, expose and represent budding talents are virtually non-existent in the film industry and the ones operational in the music industry are not well-positioned. Thus, theatre entrepreneurs could explore these opportunities by providing their services as production, artists or events managers.

Film And Videography

Film has been described as "a representation of the economic, social, political, religious, technological and cultural development of the producing country" (Ayakoroma, 2014, p.5). It is a product that "communicates information and ideas; take the viewers on a journey, offering them a patterned experience that engages their minds and emotions" (Bordewell &Thompson, 2004 p.3). As a medium that combine both sound and moving images, film has been asserted to have a uniquely powerful ubiquity within human culture (Sherak cited in Yuan, n.d.). This is because as noted by Eze-Orji (2016:108), video films usually "x-ray a particular culture and within the content and form, an aggregate of the people's social attitude in formed." The film medium is endowed with the ability to transform, superimpose, socialize and create new social order in the receiving ground (Idogho, 2016). It could as well help shape society; re-orientate the people while also entertaining them. (Farinde, 2008). Nwazue and Morison (2016) indicate that "films are mostly made or produced in the hope that viewers or consumers pay to watch or as in the case of Nollywood, buy to watch at them convenience" (p. 66). Thus, as a business enterprise that draws patronage form the masses, the emergence of Nollywood has created entrepreneurial opportunities for wide-ranging investors including photographers and videographers. Theatre graduates proficient in the art and practice of composing, capturing and recording of pictures either still or moving could venture into film making (either short or feature films). Also, those that are good at video/film cutting and assemblage could set up studios or editing suites for this purpose. The remarkable thing is that these activities could be done with or using appropriate software or applications on a computer system or laptop. Photographers and videographers could also explore the opportunities available in the coverage of events such as weddings, burials, child dedication, political rallies and so on.

Conclusion

Entrepreneurship plays a vital role in the economic development, wealth creation, employment generation and talent development. However, this is only made possible if existing economic opportunities within the environment are discovered, evaluated and exploited in view of creating goods and services for customers and maximising profit from the business venture. The task of identifying or recognizing these opportunities and mobilizing resources to take advantages of them is a critical one that must be carried out only after necessary evaluations or risks assessment have been done by the investor or entrepreneur and the identified opportunities adjudged viable. This paper has explored the theatre arts discipline to establish the networks of viable entrepreneurial opportunities embedded in theatre practice, entertainment or cultural and creative arts industry. It is the contention of this paper that if investors are encouraged to explore the full potentials or opportunities embedded in this sector of the Nigerian economy via appropriate governmental policy and funding, the economic multiplier effects accruable from such investments could revive and help pull the nation's economy out of recession.

References

Achoakawa, A. O. (2015). Postmodern directorial approaches for restoring theatre patronage in Nigeria: An experimentation with Esiaba Irobi's "Hangmen also die." An unpublished dissertation. Calabar: University of Calabar.

Achoakawa, A. O. (2014). Theatre for development as participatory research. In E. Andrew (Ed.) *Research in the human-*

ities: Dynamics in the management of knowledge creation, pp. 31-39. Lagos: Desmark Media Limited.

Agoma, A. (2016). Solo performance: The intractability and inadequacies of talent in an evolving stage. In N. Aniukwu (Ed.) *Book of proceedings - SONTA 29th Annual International Conference*, Awka.

Akpan, M (2013). Pattern composition and costume design for the theatre. *The Parnassus.* 9 (1). 171-181.

Andrew-Essien, E., & Orim, E. (2014). A comparative overview of PRA and TfD as interactive methods of data collection in humanities research. In E. Andrew (Ed.), op. cit., pp.51-61.

Anjorin, O.G. (2016). Actuating the ingenious impulse in the Nigerians child through creative dramatics. In N. Aniukwu (Ed.), op. cit., pp. 21-30.

Apeh, C (2011). Developing effective marketing strategies for Calabar university theatre productions. *Applause: Journal of Theatre and Media Studies.* 2 (1). 141-148.

Ardichvili, A., Cardozo, R., & Ray, S. (2003). A theory of entrepreneurial opportunity identification and development. *Journal of Business Venturing.* 18. 105-123.

Awodiya, M. P. (2006). *Managing arts institutions in Nigeria.* Ibadan: Kraft Book Limited.

Ayakoroma, B. (2012). Theatre practice in Nigeria: To be or not to be. Keynote Address presented at International Theatre Day, Abuja.

Ayakoroma, B. (2014). Re-inventing the political process in Nigerian films: A critical reading of Teco Benson's "The Senator." *Nigerian Theatre Journal.* 14 (2). 1-21.

Bade-Afuye, T. B. (2015). The impact of costume and make-up in Yoruba video film. Retrieved, June 15, 2017 from http://www.sonta.nico.gov.ng/index...phyp/papers/342.

Bhave, M. (1994). A process model of entrepreneurial venture creation. *Journal of Business Venturing.* (2). 223-242.

Barranger, M. S. (1984). *Theatre past and present: An introduction.* California: Wadsworth.

Betiang, L. (2001). *Fundamentals of dramatic literature.* Calabar:

Baarj & Omnix International Limited.

Bordewell, D., & Thompson, K. (2004). *Film art: An introduction.* (4th ed.). New York: McGraw Hill.

Bolton, G. (1998). *Acting in classroom drama.* London: Trentham Books.

Breed, A. (2002). Playback in theatre for development. Centre for Playback Theatre. Retrieved, June 15, 2017 from http://www.fenteforplaybacktheatre.org.

Brockett, O. G., & Ball, R. J. (2014). *The essential theatre.* (8th ed.). Belmont, C.A: Wadsworth/ Thomson Learning.

Burns, E. (1973). *Theatricality: A study of conventions in the theatre and social life.* London: Longman.

Cairney, S. (2001). *Solo performers: An international registry, 1770 – 2000.* London: McFarland & Company Inc.

Catrin, L. (2000). *The power of one: The solo play for playwrights, actors and directors.* Portsmouth: Heinemann.

Common, T. (1997). *Basic marketing: Principles and practice.* (4th ed.). London: Castle Publisher Ltd.

Darren, L., Conrad, L. (2009). *Entrepreneurship and small business management in the hospitality industry.* London: Elsevier.

De Koning, A. (1999). Conceptualizing opportunity recognition as a socio-cognitive process. Stockholm: Centre for Advanced Studies in Leadership.

Dubin, R. (1978). *Theory building.* (2nd ed.). New York: The Free Press.

Edet, E., & Oqua, K. (2008). Enhancing internal financial control in theatre establishment in Nigeria. *NDUNODE: Calabar Journal of the Humanities.* 7 (1). 61-75.

Ekweariri, C. S. (2014). Marketing the arts through effective branding and packaging techniques in Nigeria: The role of designers. In S. E. Ododo and O. A. Fosudo (Eds.). *Marketing Contemporary Theatre and Cultural Entertainment*, pp. 94-103. Lagos: SONTA/Concept Publications Limited.

Evans, J. R., & Berman, B. *Marketing.* New York: Macmillan Publishing Company.

Eze-Orji, B. (2016). Misrepresentation and image bastardisation of the Igbo in Nollywood films. *Nigerian Theatre Journal*. 6. 108-125.

Fasoranti, A. (2011). A study of Julie Okoh as a Nigerian female playwright-director. *Performer: Ilorin Journal of Performing Arts*. 13. 58-66.

Fleming, M. (1995). *Starting Drama Teaching*. London: David Fulton Publishers.

Folarin, A. (1985). Modern scenography in western Nigeria. *Nigeria Magazine*. 53 (3). 14-24.

Fosudo, O. A. (2014). The nature of theatre marketing: Concepts, opportunities and challenges in the selling of intangible products and services. In S. E. Ododo and O. A. Fosudo (Eds.), op. cit. pp. 23-44.

Frimpong, N. (2013). The study or drama in tertiary institutions: Prospects and challenges on students for future careers. *The Parnassus*. 9 (1). 308-323.

Gillete, M. J. (2002). *Theatrical design and production*. (4th ed.). Boston: McGraw Hill Companies.

Idiahi, E. (2011). Nigeria's creative industries: Optimising the economic potentials of the creative industry through global partnership. National Economic Summit Group.

Idogho, J. A. (2016). Theatre/drama-in-education and multimedia intervention: Perceptions and the changes in 21st century learning. In N. Aniukwu (Ed.), op. cit., pp. 508-520.

Idogho, J. A. (2016). Cultural hybirdization, feminism, and social change crusade in Nollywood: An analysis of reloaded. *Nigerian Theatre Journal*. 16. 49-64.

Idogho, J. A. (2013). Drama/theatre in education and theatre as an academic discipline: A question of nomenclature, techniques and effects. *AFFREVJAH*. 2 (3). 228-248.

Idung, P. A. (2016). Management strategies in Ibom Tropicana and Entertainment Centre. An Unpublished M. A. Dissertation, University of Uyo.

Inyang, O. (2015). Theatre and water pollution mitigation in rural communities in Nigeria: A post-intervention report of Esuk Ewang and Ibaka environmental theatre project. *The*

Artist Journal. 1 (1). 1-10.

Inyang, O. (2016). *Introduction to theatre and media practice: A beginner's guide.* Lagos: Bezeliel Publishers.

Inyang, O., Morison, G. I. (2016). The prospects of theatre for development in change communication and advocacy in rural Nigeria: A framework for action. N. Aniukwu (Ed.), op. cit. pp.122-135.

James, I. S. (2016). Playwright as psychologist and revolutionary: Dugga's "Hope Harvesters and A Bridge of Strings" as paradigm. In N. Aniukwu (Ed.). ibid. pp. 158-167.

Langley, S. (1980). *Theatre management in America: Principle and practice.* New York: Drama Books Publishers.

Light, H. R. (1982). *The nature of management.* London: Pitman.

Lucey, T. (1987). *Management Information System.* 5th ed. London: D P Publications Ltd.

Lucky, E. O. (2014). Entrepreneurship in the arts: A critical study of potentially profitable creative ventures. In N. Aniukwu (Ed.). op. cit., pp. 138-156.

Nnachi, F. O. (2016). The directional challenges in a one-man theatre: A study of Greg Mbajiorgu's "The Prime Minister's Son." An unpublished M. A. dissertation. University of Calabar.

Nwamuo, C. (2003). *Essentials of theatre administration.* Calabar: University of Calabar Press.

Nwamuo, C. (2014). Marketing the contemporary Nigerian theatre and culture entertainment. In S. E. Ododo and O. A. Fosudo (Eds.). op. cit. pp. 17-22.

Nwazue, U.C., & Morison, G. I. (2016). Market dynamics and its influence on film production and directing in Nollywood. *Nigerian Theatre Journal.*16. 65-82.

Nwazue, U.C. (2016). Filming for change in Nollywood: An experimentation with Ifufe. In N. Aniukwu. (Ed.). pp. 141-151. *Book of proceedings SONTA 29th annual international conference*, Awka.

Obongko, E., & Onwuka, E. (2016). The place of dance and music in democracy in Nigeria: Looking at the centenary multimedia show. *Nigerian Theatre Journal.* 16. 92-107.

Offoboche, E. (1998). *Drama with and for children.* Calabar: Uptriko Press.

Ogunbiyi. Y. (1981). Nigerian theatre and drama: A critical profile. *Drama and theatre in Nigeria: A critical source book.* Lagos: Nigeria Magazine.

Ogundele, O. G. (2007). *Introduction to entrepreneurship development, corporate government and small business management.* Lagos: Molofin Nominees.

Ogundeji, T. (2016). Security and the dearth of live theatre in Nigeria. *Mediterranean Journal of Social Science.* 7 (2). 238-243.

Ogu-Raphael, I. (2009). The medium of theatre as an alternative conflict resolution mechanism: A case of the Niger Delta. *Unizik Journal of Arts and Humanities.* 10 (2). 63-76.

Ohiri, I. (1999). *The basics of theatre management.* Enugu: Commercial Printing & Publishers.

Ohiri, I. (2005). Discouraging over reliance on gate takings for better theatrical business directions: A saving grace for contemporary theatre practice. *Nigerian Theatre Journal.* 8 (1). 146-156.

Ojo, B. (2004). *Rudiments of choreography* (Ed.). Lagos: Dat & Partners Logistics Ltd.

Okeke, T.J. (2016). Scenography and societal change: An appraisal of scenographic practice in a developing economy. Aniukwu (Ed.). op. cit. pp. 113-121.

Oluwafemi, J. A. (2016). Communicative and expressive value of Bata dance in contemporary Nigeria. In N. Aniukwu (Ed.). *Book of proceedings SONTA 29th Annual International Conference.* Awka. 451-450.

Postin-Anderson, B. (2008). *Drama: Learning connection in primary schools.* Oxford: Oxford University Press.

Pride, W. M., & Ferrel, E. O. (1995). *Marketing: Concepts and strategies.* Boston: Hougton Mifflin Company.

Rea, P. W., & Irving, D. K. (2001). *Producing and directing the short film and video.* London: Heinemann.

Rebecca, E. O., & Benjamin, J. I. (2009). Entrepreneurial competencies: The missing links to successful entrepreneurship in Nigeria. *International Business Research*. 2(2). 62-71.

Sirgist, B. (1999). Entrepreneurial opportunity recognition. A presentation at the Annual UIC/AMA Symposium at Marketing/Entrepreneurship Interface, Sophia-Antipolis, France.

Smiley, S. (1971). *Playwriting: The structure of actions*. London: Yale University Press.

Stevenson, H. H., Roberts, M. J., & Grousbeck, H. I. (1985). New Business Ventures and the Entrepreneur. Irvin, IL: Homewood.

The Children's Theatre Association of America. Retrieved, June 15, 2017 from www.childrenstheatreassociationofamerica.org

Tume, F. K. (2014). The use of dance in Nollywood films. *Nigerian Theatre Journal*. 16. 27-48.

Umukoro, M. (2002). *Drama and theatre in Nigerian schools*. Ibadan: Caltop Publication.

Utoh-Ezeajugh, T. (2000). Promoting minority cultures through costume and make-up: Sam Ukala's *Break in Production*. A. D. Asasba (Ed). *Theatre and minority rights: Perspectives in the Niger Delta*. pp. 129-141. Ibadan: Kraft Book Ltd. 129-141.

Ventakaraman, S. (1997). The distinctive domain of entrepreneurship research: An editor's perspective. J. Katz and R. Brockhens (Eds.) *Advances in entrepreneurship, firm emergence, and growth*. Vol. 3, pp.119-138.

Wagner, J. B. (1998). *Educational drama and language arts: What research shows?* Portsmouth: Heinemann.

Walliman, N. (2011). *Research methods: The basics*. New York: Routledge.

Wessels, C. (1987). *Drama*. Oxford: Oxford University Press.

Wilson, E. (2004). *The theatre experience*. (9[th]ed.). New York: McGraw Hill Companies.

Yalokwu, P.O. (2002). *Fundamentals of management*. Lagos: Peak Publishers.

Yuan, L. (n.d). How movies affect society. Retrieved, June 15,

2017   from___http://www.academia.edu/....how-movies-affect-society.html.

gdy4life@gmail.com

CHAPTER 6

ENTREPRENEURSHIP SKILLS IN VOCATIONAL AND TECHNICAL EDUCATION FOR NATIONAL DEVELOPMENT IN NIGERIA

U. G. THOMAS, R. O. NAIBI, D. C. UDOJI, E. ENYIEBI,
S. O. GEORGE, & F. ONOTANIYHOWO.
Department of Fine and Applied Arts
Federal College of Education (Technical)
Omoku, Nigeria.

Abstract

The human resources needed to transform Nigeria's economy must be adequately skilled through quality entrepreneurship education. It is imperative to involve Nigerian youths in vocational/technical education (VTE) to acquire capabilities that will help them realize their innate abilities for self-reliance. This paper examines concepts related to entrepreneurship, vocational and technical education, and issues connected with the two.

Keywords: Entrepreneurship, Vocational and Technical Education, National Development

Introduction

A ttainment of self-reliance through entrepreneurial skills is vital to every developing economy. Vocational and technical training is geared towards acquisition of practical skills, competencies, attitudes, and knowledge relating to occupation in various sectors of the economy and social life. The vocational and technical courses such as Fine and Applied Arts Education, Agricultural Education, Home Economics, Business Education, Automobile, Woodwork, Metalwork, Electrical/Electronics, Building Technology are packaged to provide practical skills for attaining self-reliance.

Entrepreneurship in the opinion of Ezemuo, Offor and Ezeudu (2013) is a process of generating ideas and venturing into business, taking the risks created by the dynamic environment and making the best of opportunities available to make profit. This means that an entrepreneur is a person who assumes the responsibility and the risk for a business operation with the expectation of making profit. Is there a link between vocational/technical education and entrepreneurship? The answer is in the positive, and vocational/technical education goes beyond that to include preparation of students for several occupations in the arts and sciences field.

Vocational/technical education as indicated by Okoro (1999) is a form of education with the primary purpose of equipping the learner with skills, knowledge, and attitudes for employment in specific and recognized occupation. Akanuwor (1988) notes that that the bed rock of any technical breakthrough is the existence of appropriate skills, abilities, and competencies both mental and physical as equipment for the individual to live in the society. Thus, Kurya and Hassan (2007) state that "Vocational and technological education is a programme designed to equip learners with vocational skills for employment in various fields of human endeavor."

Bulus (1991) views vocational technical education as the acquisition of skills and competencies that can help individuals to function productively in industries and commercial occupation. Enahoro (2008) holds that vocational training is utilitarianism and is a concept recognizing the importance of labour. "The idea of vocational education is that it combines education and training for the purpose of work; it is an education in which skills are taught for the purpose of gaining employment through exposure to practical experience for self-actualization" (Legg-Jack, Idibia, & Onyije, 2013).

Areas Of Training In Vocational And Technical Education (Vte)

In vocational/technical education, students/youths can undergo training in specializations such as:

1. Fine and Applied Arts Education: Training in this vocation exposes students to skills in drawing, painting, sculpture, photography, graphics and design, textiles, and ceramics.
2. Agricultural Education: Training for job on the farms and occupation in such fields as food processing, marketing of farm products, and repairing of farm equipment.
3. Home Economics Education: Training for home making and for occupations in such fields as child care, food management, and interior decoration.
4. Business Education: Training for distributive and office occupations. Distributive education covers such subjects as merchandizing, warehousing, and export-import trade. Office education includes such subjects as typewriting, bookkeeping, use of business machines, and shorthand.
5. Technical Education: Training in this area gives skill in woodwork, automobile, building, electrical/elec-

tronics.

With respect to Fine and Applied Arts Education, White in Naibi, George, Thomas and Nwaoloko (2015) states that art education courses include advertising, antique appraisal, fashion design, costume design, art teaching, architectural design, portraiture, web design, photography, museum management, gallery management, textile and clothing, pot making, utensils and vase making, book printing, posters and hand bill printing among others. Specific entrepreneurial areas of specialization include:

Drawing: The art of using pencil, charcoal, ink, pastel, marker or any drawing media to draw on paper, board, or any flat surface. Skills derived from this can make one independent in life.

Painting: This has to do with the use of brushes, spatula, palette knife, spray-gun to apply colours (paint – oil, acrylic, water, pastel) in a painterly form on canvas or support. It could be portrait painting, seascape, market scene, festivals or any other concept as the client demands.

Graphics and Design: This relates to the use of words (letters) and sometime images (photographs) to send or communicate ideas especially for commercial purposes. This could be done manually or digitally with the computers. Graphic designers create logos, books, magazines, packages, posters, web sites, film titles, signage, and other media (Ellen, 2006). Students that acquire skills in this field can take up career in advertising, television, marketing and print media, among other vocations. Orifa (2002) notes that a graphic designer must be concerned not only with product and packaging design but with the conditions under which products are sold, that is, the scope of a graphics designer is wider than just designing and packaging.

Ceramics/Pottery: This field enables a student to acquire skills in the use of clay and other pottery making materials to build jugs, flower vases, teacups, plates, pots, trinkets, ceramic sculptures, flasks for aesthetics and commercial purposes.

Textiles: Textiles prepares students in skills related to fabric and leather making such as weaving, tie-dye, batik, sewing, and embroidery.

Sculpture /Three-Dimensional Art: Sculpture introduces students to moulding, casting, and carving using different media. Students gain skills in the use of metal, wood, clay, fiber, resin, concrete, stones, weaving (cane, basket, mat, rug, straw weaving, and calabash decoration. Ibrahim (2000) recognizes black-smiting as a craft which people take pride in where practiced. This means that black-smiting is also a skill that is available in the field of arts.

Photography: This is another field in art that is very lucrative and competitive in the society today. It involves the use of photographic gadgets such as the camera (digital) and its accessories to snap images for documentation or commercialization. Training in photography provides skills and job in the movies, advertising, journalism, sciences (marine and space), medical, military, oil industries and other institutions.

Careers in arts now have brought a great demand for technical training in them. However, some information about graphic art, industrial design, and commercial art can help throw light on some professional opportunities that are open to art students (Uzoagba, 1978). Successful acquisition of these entrepreneurial skill makes the beneficiaries relevant in different occupations, involvement in sale of artworks, art materials, commissioned jobs, mentoring or tutorial (apprenticeship), own gallery and host of art exhibition.

Prospects Of Vocational And Technical Education In Nigeria

Vocational/technical education (VTE) is a form of education specifically designed to meet the economic and social needs of young individuals who want to acquire job competencies and also become entrepreneurs. As articulated by Obioma (2010) in Obiyai and Ehimen (2013) there are enormous prospects as follows:

1. The reform policies of the Nigerian Government recognize education as an instrument par excellence for social and economic transformation and attaining the goals of Vision 2020; this has been transforming the country's economy. A critical success factor in the actualization of Nigeria's Vision 2020 is the mass production of people with requisite vocational and technical skills and competencies. VTE is designed to train and impact individuals with necessary skills and competencies leading to the production of craftsmen, technicians and technologists who will be enterprising and self-reliant, thus having the potentials to employ others and reduce poverty.

2. The planned scaling up of the establishment of Vocational Enterprise Institute (VEI's) will facilitate the training and mass production of middle level manpower required for job creation, wealth generation, and reduction of poverty. This will provide life-long education for youths who may not be able to proceed beyond junior or senior secondary education.

3. Nigeria, for now, lacks highly skilled manpower needed in modern industries. The activities in the oil and gas sector must meet and overcome challenges of lack of indigenous manpower, otherwise, they will continue to rely on foreign expertise. We must be able to develop local human capital that will meet local needs and at the same time satisfy international skills bench marks required for the oil sector and the emerging industries.

4. The National Vocational Qualification Framework (NVQF) if entrenched, will link work and industry. The NVQF places emphasis on competencies and functional skills rather than on paper qualification. It will also facilitate the generation and application of a more realistic reward system for employees.

5. Presidential Summit on Education (PSE) provides greater opportunities for improvement of TVET and the attendant impact on social and economic development. With the planned restructuring of the school system and the ensuing content standards, opportunities have been opened for innovation and improvements that will meet local needs as well as global technological competitiveness.

In line with this, UNESCO (2004) pointed out that since education is considered the key to effective development strategies of all forms, VTE must be the master key that can alleviate poverty, promote peace, conserve the environment, improve the quality of life for all and help achieve sustainable development.

Recommendations

1. There is need for government to build more vocational and technical colleges, centers and industries and engage the youths.
2. Financial institutions in Nigeria should provide soft loans to young graduates to establish small scale industries, art studios and galleries as this will encourage and increase interest of many individuals in vocational technical education.
3. Training and re-training of vocational technical teachers should be made paramount, sponsored and monitored for effective delivery.
4. Federal government should increase its funding to vocational and technical education institutions in Nigeria as the cost of technology increases with time.

Conclusion

The ability of Nigeria to realize the Millennium Development Goals (MDGs) is dependent on its capacity to transform its populace into highly skilled and competent entrepreneurial individuals. To achieve this lies in the productivity of its citizens through quality and affordable vocational and technical education program. VTE is the master key that can provide the quality and affordable entrepreneurial education that can impart skills, knowledge, abilities and competencies leading to self-reliant potentials and generate employment for others as well alleviate poverty in Nigeria.

References

Alaba, O. (2006). Financing your business through SMEEIS fund: Banking. *Broad Street Journal.*

Anene, G. U. (2002). Vocational education as a tool for self-reliance. *Journal of Technical Education Research and Development.* 2. 83-88.

Akanuwor, K. I. (1988). Instructional materials in vocational-technical education. Paper presented at the 16th Annual Conference of the Vocational Association, University of Uyo.

Ibrahim, B. (2000). Visual arts made easy for schools and colleges. Lagos: Movic Publishing.

Bassey, I. E. (2009). Recreating primary education for patriotism and self-reliant: Implication for teacher education. *Journal of Quality Education.* 5 (1).

Bulus, F. (1991). Guidance practice in schools. Jos: Ehindero (Nig.) Limited.

Ejimaji, E. U., Ekpa, M. M. M., and Ellah, A. D. (2009). Quality education for women empowerment. *Journal of Contemporary Business and Educational Research.* 2(1).

Ellen, l. (2006). Design it yourself: A design handbook. New York: Princeton Architectural Press.

Etuk, A. G. (2013). Guidance and counseling in vocational technical education in Nigerian schools. *Journal of Technical Technology and Vocational Educators.* 3 (1). 104-112.

Enahoro, N. I. (2008). Technical and vocational education for productivity and sustainable development in Nigeria. *International Journal of Research* 1(1&2).

Ezemuo, D. T., Offor, I. C., & Ezeudu, A. I. (2013). Creativity in entrepreneurial development: Implication in national development.

Federal Republic of Nigeria (2004). National policy on education. (4ᵗʰ ed.). Yaba: NERDC Press.

sustainable development in Nigeria. Proceedings of the 20ᵗʰ Annual National Conference of National Association of Teachers of Technology (NATT) held at Kaduna Polytechnic, Kaduna, 5ᵗʰ-7ᵗʰ October.

Legg-Jack, D. W., Idibia, C. N., & Onyije, D. (2013). Youth empowerment through a revitalized technical and vocational education and training for sustainable national development. *Journal of Technical and Vocational Educators.* 3 (1). 46-53.

Naibi, R. O., George, S.O., Thomas, U. G & Nwaoloko, J. U. (2015). Re-positioning art education for entrepreneurship among youths for self-employment. *Nigerian Journal of education, science and technology.* 2 (2). 53-61.

Nwogu, P. O. (2009). The global economic crisis: A challenge to entrepreneurship development in technical and vocational education and training (TVET). Paper presented at the 22ⁿᵈ Annual National Conference of NATT at Bauchi, October 17ᵗʰ-21ˢᵗ, 2009

Obiyai, K. K., & Ehimen, T. E. (2013). Trends in improving the Nigerian workforce through technical vocational and training (TVET). *Journal of Technical Technology and Vocational Educators.* 3 (1). 120-127.

Okoro, O. M. (199). Principles and methods in vocational and technical education. Onitsha: University Trust Publishers.

Olaitan, S. O., Onyemachi, G. A., & Nwachukwu, C. (2000). Poverty and poverty alleviation initiatives in Nigeria. Nsukka: Ndudim Printing Press.

Orifa, C. O. (2002). *Creative arts: A tool for effective marketing strategy*. Paper presented at the National Association for Visual Arts Education held at Warri.

Raymond, E. (2007). *Constraints affecting electronics of roadside technicians in Minna metropolis*: JONATT 6(2).

UNESCO, (2004). Analytical Survey: The use of ICT in Technology and Vocational Education and Training (TVET). Mosco: Institute for Information Technologies Education.

Uzoagba, I. N. (1978). *Understanding art in general education*. Africana Educational Publishers (Nigeria) Ltd, Onitsha.

CHAPTER 7

ENTREPRENEURSHIP COUNSELLING: A VERITABLE TOOL FOR PROMOTING VOCATIONAL EDUCATION AND ECONOMIC DEVELOPMENT AT SECONDARY SCHOOLS IN NIGERIA

Allen Chuks ONYIJE
Tuzi Dickens EWE(Mrs.)
Federal College of Education (Technical), Omoku, Rivers State

Abstract

The Federal government in the national policy on secondary education makes provision for students to become vocationally oriented while in school to prepare them for self-reliance when they are through with school life. But the plans lacked the ability to achieve this purpose. This paper discusses the place of counselling in achieving the plans made by government with respect to helping secondary school students to gain insight into the world of work by of entrepreneurship education at that level of education. The rationale for skill development is to shift emphasis on crude oil which may dry up any time and counselling plays a vital role in this regard.

Keywords: Vocational Education, Counselling, Economic Development, Self-Reliance, Entrepreneurship, Skills

Introduction

Secondary school education is the type of education for young individuals of about 13-17 years of age. The objectives of secondary education are to provide technical and vocational competencies in vocational subjects such as agriculture, creative arts, home economics, industrial, commercial, and economic development (FRN, 2004). But secondary education in Nigeria seems not to meet these demands. It is observed that secondary school leavers roam about the streets unable to be employed or employable. Thus, Omioregie in Ifeanacho and Ifeanacho (2014) laments that secondary school graduates cannot live useful lives in the society because of the over-emphasis on theory. It is also noted that secondary leavers cannot work or be self-employed because the necessary skills needed to prepare them for employment were not available to them when they were school.

Since crude oil price in the world market has dwindled dramatically, there is the need youths in secondary schools to acquire skills to fortify themselves for the future when paid employment will be scarcer. Knowledge and skills become paramount and such can be made available through vocational education. Counselling is critical at this stage.

Career education is an emphasis in education, which seeks to make school experiences more related to experiences in the world of work. It is a process of facilitating career development in all students by modifying school educational experiences as well as experiences in the industrial sector and home (Nwadinobi, Umezulike, & Eneasator, 2013). This implies that career education is the continuous quest of helping individuals to choose occupations, prepare for them, enter them, and remain in them consistently. The emphasis here is on career/ vocational awareness and preparation to face realities of world of work by secondary school students before and after graduation.

Entrepreneurship education on the other hand is the involvement of abilities to set up business enterprises and operate them successfully. Such abilities should be acquired and should differ in some respects than the abilities required for paid employment. It involves the acquisition of skills, ideas, and managerial abilities necessary for personal self-reliance. Self–reliance of an individual relates to the ability to set one's own goals and realizing them as much as possible through one's efforts using one's own resources. This personal or individual self-reliance effort when put together can transform into national self-reliance because when the individual is gainfully productive through self-employment, the nation is positively affected. The entrepreneurship concern in this paper, therefore must be the type which inculcates the skills of a technological nature and the skills of floating and succeeding in a business enterprise which can commence from the secondary school level.

It is the duty of schools to provide youths in secondary schools with the educational experiences relevant to their future vocational plans (Osuala, 1976). It is also the responsibility of the technical schools in particular to provide training for competence in specific occupations. What is worrisome is that the schools and colleges in Nigeria have remained too theoretical, emphasizing basic rather than applied knowledge.

Vocational education is a tool for promoting entrepreneurship at the secondary school level for economic development in an economy. It can be a tool to position Nigerians for life after crude oil. Entrepreneurship and vocational education are in common in providing and training manpower of different professional grades that will aid and support government in solving some national issues such as unemployment, social vices, and so on. Entrepreneurship education is not only related to teaching individuals to own and manage businesses, it involves encouraging creative thinking and promoting a strong sense of self-worth and accountability (Nwadike, Godwins, Amaewhule, & Orakwelu, 2016).

Strategies For Encouraging Entrepreneurship Education In Schools

Strategies to encourage entrepreneurship education in secondary schools include:

1. Building achievement motivation into learning - Esomonu (1997) explains that entrepreneurship education and learning should motivate students to seek for success in new ventures through their efforts and skills and not just by chance. If the achievement motives and achievement value are developed among larger number of Nigerian youths, the environment should be expected to experience a rapid economic and individual development.

2. Model quality performance – Successful entrepreneurs within and outside the country should be invited to lecture students on entrepreneurship adventures. Just like the venture This is what Governor Ikpeazu of Abia State did in April 2017 when he invited entrepreneurs from China to teach Abia State youths how to produce quality shoes and other products.

3. Management efficiency courses - Entrepreneurship education is expected to emphasize tools for good management of enterprises.

    1. Research and motivation - No strategies directed towards indigenous economic growth and industrial development can afford to neglect investments in research because it is through research that innovation emerges.

Entrepreneurship Counselling

Vocational counselling is an assistance rendered to individuals to solve problems related to choice of career. It is an effort made by the counsellor to sublimate the individual with wrong views about vocations or who have no knowledge or little ideas about vocations so that maximum information can be provided to enable them to make right choices. The ultimate choice is still the secondary school students who through vocational counselling gain insight that enables them set realistic goals which attainment will be within their reach and ability. The counsellor has a critical part to play in the process. These, as Iruloh, Ernest-Ehibudu, and Onuorah (2016) explain, include:

1. to help the individual student order his experiences
2. help him to define his goals
3. help him to define his values
4. help him to define his aspirations (p. 27).

Counselling on its own plays three distinct roles by being:

1. a helping relationship
2. a talking therapy
3. a learning experience

Irulor, et al (2016) also indicate that as a talking therapy, counselling helps in the lifting up burdened, frustrated, and depressed minds to achieve stability and participate meaningfully in opportunities available. As a learning experience, it affords both counsellor and client the opportunity of ordering their experiences by engaging in alternative behaviours that offer better dividends. It is through guidance and counselling that people including students review or reassess their previous experiences for a more rewarding life style. The application of encouragement enables a person to develop image for self through self-understanding, self-direction, and through acquisition of skills in problem-solving and decision-making situations.

Need For Counselling Secondary School Students For Entrepreneurship Skills

The primary purpose of entrepreneurship counselling is to convince, encourage, and restructure the understanding and intellect of students towards skills while they are young. It can also create opportunities for discovering hidden talents and abilities during which jobs and individuals are matched (Parsons in Ikenyiri, 2017). Rsehi in Nwadike et al (2016) notes that there is need to introduce and strengthen counselling services in schools to meet the various aspirations of the students in skill acquisition. The school system can collaborate with government at all levels in ensuring that entrepreneurship education is success. This can lead to diversification of the Nigerian economy which is currently a mono-product economy.

Strategies For Enhancing Entrepreneurship Education

The following steps will be necessary in enhancing entrepreneurship training of secondary school students:

1. Entrepreneurship education and training for self-employment should be made available to students through vocational education programmes at the secondary school level. Esomonu (1997) suggests that the concept of owning and operating a small-scale business should be established in career education programme at that level.

2. To provide education and training to meet the specific needs of students for self-employment, new methods and concepts of delivering instruction will need to be explored. The teacher is required to lay the foundation of technological/skill development for any nation. Both the quality and pace of skill advancement

depends on the quality and efficiency of the teacher. He is expected to be trained to improve in his quality of instruction as it concerns vocational skills.

3   The implementation of entrepreneurship education within vocational education programmes calls for development and effective utilization of instructional materials such as textbooks, and others. It is important for the practitioner in the field and government to partner to develop relevant textbooks and relevant instructional materials for effective instructions in entrepreneurship education within the vocation education programmes.

4   Secondary school authorities are expected to attach their students once in a while to business enterprises within their environment for hands-on experiences. This programme is on-going in tertiary institutions of learning. It is vital to develop ways of working with other agencies, institutions and organizations ready to provide training and assistance to small business.

5   Industrial work experiences for students is existing in tertiary institutions of learning but is lacking in secondary grammar schools. The schools are expected to work closely with the industries and industrial training fund (ITF) to ensure that students secure establishments where exposure to necessary skills in real work situations are available to them before graduation.

Problems Of Entrepreneurship Education

The following are some of the problems encountered while administering entrepreneurship education in secondary schools:

1.   Trained personnel - few people have the professional skills in entrepreneurship education; the available few prefer industries where remunerations are better.

2.   There is inadequacy of instructional materials to use in teaching skills in secondary schools.

3.   The cost of establishing businesses in Nigeria is so

high that the poor can hardly venture into viable businesses. Loans from banks are not easily accessible by people and certainly not including secondary school students.

4. Government policies are not friendly; they create hindrances for effective skill development.

5. Electrical power is a sine-qua-non to developing business enterprises. Electric power supply in Nigeria in Nigeria is on a serious hindrance to business development.

6. Others include insecurity, poor means of transportation, lack of storage systems and facilities, ignorance about entrepreneurship skills, and lack of interest in skill acquisition and development by youths.

Conclusion

Entrepreneurship skill education creates necessary awareness and motivations in students for promotion of self-employment and societal development. Positive attitude towards entrepreneurship must be inculcated in students by counselling through guidance counsellors who have the expertise to develop the potential abilities of individuals. Counselling helps the students to over-haul themselves and create self-understanding, self-direction, and decision making. Entrepreneurship education at various levels for self-employment, local/special programmes for entrepreneurship growth, the effective implementation of entrepreneurship education within vocational education programmes are some of the strategies for enhancing entrepreneurship education. The lack of trained personnel, funds, material instruments, insecurity, ignorance about entrepreneurship education in schools among others are impediments experienced by entrepreneurship education and guidance counsellors in Nigeria.

References

Esomonu, N. P. M. (1997). *Entrepreneurship practice in education.* Umunze: Federal College of Education (Technical).

Federal Republic of Nigeria (2004). *National policy on education.* Abuja: NERDC Press.

Ikenyiri, E. (2017). *Guidance and counseling: Principles and practice (2nd. ed).* Omoku: Jeff Publishing Company.

Ifenacho, V. A., & Ifenacho, J. C. (2014). Secondary schools entrepreneurship education: An imperative for entrepreneurship development, job creation, wealth generation, and global competitiveness. *Journal of Faculty of Education, Ignatius Ajuru University of Education.* 13 (1). 211-221.

Iruloh, B. I., Ernest-Ehibudu, I. R., & Onuorah, M. N. (2016). Encouraging communication, collaboration and creative action among Niger Delta youths for better socio-economic adjustment to life: Implications for adjusting to life after oil. *Rivers State Counselling Association of Nigeria Journal.* 2 (1). 23-33

Nwadike, I. S., Godwins, M., Amaewhule, E. C., & Orakwelu, U. (2016). Entrepreneurship counseling and role of vocational education in promoting entrepreneurship in secondary schools for economic development of Nigeria. ibid. 279-289.

Nwadinobi, V.N., Umezulike, R. Q., & Eneasator, U. E. (2013). *Educational information and vocational development in counselling: A theoretical approach.* Onitsha: The Light of Winners.

Otobo, P., & Alabi, E. B. (2016). Entrepreneurship education for self-reliance among graduates of tertiary institutions in Nigeria: The role of counseling. op. cit. 105-113.

Osuala, E. C. (1998). *Foundation of vocational education.* Onitsha: Cape publishers Int'l limited.

CHAPTER 8

TECHNICAL AND VOCATIONAL EDUCATION: A CATALYST FOR SOCIO-ECONOMIC AND TECHNOLOGICAL DEVELOPMENT OF NIGERIA

Prince Omoregie IYAGBAYE
Federal College of Education (Technical) Omoku.

Abstract

In the quest for socio-economic development, Nigeria needs a fundamental road map which education proffers especially in this period that it is recovering from recession. This paper regards technical and vocational education as the catalyst for national development. The paper examines the concepts of national development and technical/vocational education as well as the role of technical and vocational education in national development along with the challenges of technical and vocational education in Nigeria. This paper indicates that national development is pivoted on industrialization and productivity which technical and vocational education can be used as tool to attain. Therefore, government and other stake holders should pay more attention and invest more in this direction.

Keywords: Technical and Vocational Education, Socio-Economic Development, Technological   Development, Productivity, Self-reliance.

Introduction

N ational development is the ability of a country or countries to improve the social welfare of the people by providing social amenities like quality education, potable water, transportation infrastructure, medical care, etc. The need for development in any nation cannot be over emphasized. Development is critical and essential to the sustenance and growth of any nation. A country is classified as developed when it can provide qualitative life for her citizenry. However, it has been established that technical and vocational education is a major catalyst that drives development in any nation of the world, that is, the level of technical and vocational education development or the quality of technical and vocational education of any nation is directly proportional to its level of development; as no nation can develop more than its educational system.

It is generally believed that one of the major parameters for measuring a country's economic growth, development and self-reliance is the extent of the country's development in vocational and technical education (Kehinde & Adewuyi, 2015).

Technical and vocational education is that aspect of education that imparts the necessary skills, knowledge and competencies needed for socio-economic and technological development. The relegation of technical and vocational education is injurious and tantamount to under development. Its plays a very key role in the industrialization of any country. It is on this wise that the National Policy on Education (2013) places serious emphasis on the development of vocational and technical education for overall development of the nation.

Ovbiagele (2015) states that for any developing nation, the level of economic growth is tied to the level of technology that exists therein. He continued by saying that, Technology, by this we mean the ability to improve on the ways things are done for better performance, and it is only through the application of appropriate technologies that the skillful but jobless/unemployed can be made functional in our society. Technical and vocational education is programmed to lead to the acquisition of relevant skills for self-reliance, employment and societal functionality, that is, a focus in technical and vocational education is the eradication of unemployment.

The rate of unemployment in Nigeria has contributed immensely to the under-development and economic recession experienced presently. This is a result of inadequate skilled man power (artisans, craftsmen, technicians and technologist) to drive the nation's construction and production industry. This superlative rate of unemployment has emanated from the negligence of technical and vocational education. It has been observed that, artisans and other level of skilled manpower and goods and services are now being imported into the country thereby reducing the nation's gross domestic product (GDP). Okeke (2016) notes that with the dearth of skilled workers in the construction sector, jobs hitherto meant for Nigerians have been hijacked by expatriates on a platter of gold while leaving the indigenous artisans in abject poverty. It is no longer news that the average Nigerian lives on less than a dollar per day.

The Federal Government of Nigeria is aware of the need for Technical Education in the country as a means of attaining the much-desired technological growth. This awareness is clearly reflected in the goals set for technical education as highlighted in the National Policy on Education (FRN, 2013). One of the goals of technical and vocational education is to increase the employability of school leavers. Ironically due to negligence and prejudice this goal seem not realized today, which is the cause of mass unemployment, poverty, starvation, youth restiveness and agitations, kidnapping, armed robbery and all the social vices experienced in Nigeria presently, which have slowed down national development.

The Concept Of National Development

National development refers to the ability of a nation to improve the lives of its citizens. Measures of improvement may be material, such as an increase in the gross domestic product; or social, such as literacy rates and availability of healthcare; it is the ability of a country or countries to improve the social welfare of the people by providing amenities such as quality education, potable water, transportation infrastructure, medical care, and others that constitute national development.

Development is critical and essential to the sustenance and growth of any nation. Federal governments draw up national development plans and policies based on the perceived needs of their citizens. Many include an emphasis on reducing poverty, provision of affordable, housing and community development. Tolu and Abe (2011) opined that the pride of any government is the attainment of higher value levels of development in such a way that citizens would derive natural attachment to governance. Gboyega (2003) captures development as an idea that embodies all attempts to improve the conditions of human existence in all ramifications.

National development can be viewed as the all-embracing or totality of socio-economic, educational, religious, political, health, and infrastructural improvement of a nation. This can be achieved by setting up well articulated developmental plans or strategies. The goal of all national development is to improve the lives of the citizens within the context of a growing economy and an emphasis on the good of the community.

The Concept Of Technical And Vocational Education

It is common to find the terms 'technical' and 'vocational' used compositely when they should be used in a restricted sense and vice versa. Sometimes, where the terms are used separately, conjointly or interchangeably, some individual (including intellectuals) interpret 'vocational' to mean business subjects or studies, and 'technical' to mean technical subjects or studies, or that which has to do with engine or metals. When used in relation to school, 'vocational school' is taken to mean institutions where only business subjects are taught, while technical school is taken to mean where only technical subjects are taught. This goes to support the general notion that 'vocational' means that which has to do with business studies, while 'technical' stands for that which has to do with technical studies (Kehinde & Adewuyi,

2015)

Nwadioha in Ovbiagele (2015) holds that the terms "vocational" and "technical" in relation to education are in most cases used interchangeably. However though similar, they are not the same. Vocational education is an aspect of education that lays emphasis on skills acquisition and functional education for the development of the society. That is, it leads to employment in a job, a trade or occupation. Technical education is an aspect of education which leads to the acquisition of practical and applied skills as well as basic scientific knowledge. It gives both quality and quantity of the manpower required for transformation of a country in a technical world of work. The National Policy an Education (FRN, 2013) indicates that technical and vocational education are used together as a composite term referring to those aspects of the educational process involving in addition to general education, the study of technology and related sciences and the acquisition of practical skills, attitudes, understanding and knowledge relating to occupations in various sectors of the economic and social life. It further explains the concept of vocational and technical education to imply an integral part of general education; a means of preparing for participation in world of work; an aspect of lifelong learning; a preparation for responsible citizenship; and an instrument for promoting environmentally healthy sustainable development.

Thompson (2002) opines that vocational education aims at the development of human abilities in terms of knowledge, skills, and understanding to enable individuals efficiently carry on activities of their choice for dialing living. Winer (2000) in his contribution indicates that vocational education is designed to develop skills, abilities, understanding, attitudes, work habits and appreciation encompassing knowledge and information needed by workers to enter and make progress in employment on a useful and productive basis. It is an integral part of the total education programme and contributes towards the development of good citizens by developing their physical, social civic, cultural, and economic competencies.

Technical/vocational education is therefore that aspect of education that prepares the individual for functional life. By acquiring occupational skills and competencies through technical and vocational education, the individual becomes part of national development either by setting up a small-scale business or becoming employable or is employed or becomes an employer of labour.

The Role Of Technical And Vocation Education In National Development

The secret of rapid development experience in the developed nations of the globe has technical and vocational education undertone. Nuru (2007) states that changes in a country's economy are required to prepare young people for the jobs of the future and technical and vocational education play in this process. Technical and vocational education can be a catalyst for national development with special importance in Nigeria in several ways.

First, with the fall of crude oil price in the global market, Nigeria government has taken to diversification of the economy. This involves exploring sectors of the economy other than crude oil to stimulate development. In the agricultural sector for instance, Nigerians can process their farm produce rather than exporting cash crops. To archive this, new global technological practices must be employed of which skilled manpower is needed. Technical and vocational education training (TVET) becomes a priority here.

Second, technical/vocational education is designed to prepare the individual for functional social life by helping to develop competency skills for employment in the industry or for self-employment. Preparation for self-reliance reduces dependence on government for employment as the individual becomes not only self-employed but could be an employer of labour in skill areas such as electrical/electronics, plumbing, automobile works, vulcanizing, computer engineering, GSM repairs, dress making, and so on.

Third, technical/vocational education helps to equip the trainee with employability skills needed to run industries. For development to take root in any nation, such nation must be industrialized; and the local industry should be driven by indigenous skilled manpower. But in Nigeria the reverse is the case as the industries are driven by more of foreigners. This is because technical/vocational education is not given the attention it deserves. Okeke (2016) observes that with the dearth of skilled workers in the construction sector, jobs that Nigerians should have handled are taken over by expatriates thus increasing the level of unemployment in the country. Sahel Standard (2015) points out that over the years, many foreign companies source their artisan manpower requirements from countries such as Togo and Benin Republic, leaving many Nigerians without jobs. It also notes that in Nigeria, the prevailing gap occurs due to qualitative and quantitative skills incongruity.

Fourth, Kehinde and Adewuyi (2015) state that through vocational and technical education, local technology can be developed by indigenous technicians and technologists. It should be emphasized that every society has its own peculiar problems. It should therefore take the ingenuity of local artisans, craftsmen, technicians, and technologists to design and fabricate tools, equipment, and simple or complex machines to solve local problems. This should save the nation billions of Naira or dollars in foreign currency that would have been used in importing machines, most of which break down shortly on arrival in the country because they were not designed for the tropical and business environment.

Fifth, technical/vocational education can reduce crime and social vices in the society such as robbery, drug addiction, rioting, kidnapping, among others. This would make the society friendly for investors which in turn would stimulate the economy and trigger development. This is because skills acquired through TVET could keep the youths busy and keep them off the streets.

Sixth, technical/vocational education helps to bridge the gap between theory and practice. It exposes trainees to practical and workshop experiences thereby providing them with competency skills needed to fill manpower need in the industry. In this way the individual member of the nation is developed and is equipped to contribute to the development of the society. There is no gainsaying that the survival of individuals will ensure the survival of the nation.

Challenges Of Technical And Vocational Education

Factors that militate against technical and vocational education in Nigeria include:

1. Funding: Running a technical and vocational institution is capital intensive and resources are not easy to come by.

2. Power supply: Workshop equipment and related facilities are mostly electrically powered but the epileptic power supply experienced in Nigeria is a hindrance to use of these facilities.

3. Trained/Experienced Personnel: Many of those parading themselves as teachers in technical and vocation schools lack the requisite training in the use of modern workshop machines and equipment and lack practical skills and experience to guide trainees.

4. Workshop Equipment and Facilities: Generally, technical schools in Nigeria lack workshop equipment for practical work. Where they are available, they are obsolete.

5. Maintenance Culture: Facilities and equipment in technical and vocational schools are generally in dilapidated state because of lack of routine maintenance.

6. Public Attitude: Many parents in Nigeria believe that technical/vocational education is for youths that did not do well in school and may not cope with higher education. They prefer professions such as medicine, law, engineering and others that are popular.

Recommendations

1. Public enlightenment campaign should be organized to sensitize the public on the importance of technical and vocational education.

2. Government, industries, and other organizations should partner to provide workshop facilities to tech-

nical and vocational schools.

3.   Scholarship and grants should be awarded to teachers and students interested in technical and vocational education.

4.   Budgetary allocation to technical and vocational institutions should be increased.

5.   Female students should be encouraged to study technical education by giving them scholarship.

6.   School administrators should ensure routine maintenance is done on machines available at the school workshops.

7.   There should constant power supply to technical and vocational schools.

8.   Supervisory and monitoring committees should be set up to ensure proper implementation of technical education policies.

9.   The Federal Government should ensure the establishment of more technical and vocational schools.

Conclusion

Technical and vocational education is a a major gateway to development of any nation, Nigeria inclusive. To achieve this, governments and other stakeholders should ensure proper implementation of the goals of technical and vocational education. This aspect of education needs urgent declaration of a state of emergency because a lot have really gone wrong.

There should be stocktaking of how the nation has fared in technical/vocational education and areas of lapses identified. This will help in rejuvenating technical and vocational education in Nigeria, which will in turn catalyze national development.

References

Federal Republic of Nigeria (2013). *National policy on education*, Yaba, Lagos: Nigerian Educational Research and Development Council (NERDC).

Gboyega, A. (2003). *Democracy and development: The imperative of local governance*. An Inaugural Lecture. University of Ibadan. pp.6-7.

Kehinde, T. M., & Adewuyi, L. A. (2015). Vocational and technical education: A viable tool for transformation of the Nigerian economy. *International Journal of Vocational and Technical Education Research.* 1(2). 22-31.

Nuru, A. (2017). The relevance of national vocational education qualification (NVQs) in TVE in Nigeria. Unpublished conference paper.

Okeke, C. (2016, February 13). Repositioning artisans for production in the construction industry. *Leadership Newspaper*.

Ovbiagele, A. O. (2015). Vocational education for socio-economic and technological development of Nigeria. *Global Journal of Interdisciplinary Social Sciences. 4*(4). 15-18.

Sahel Standard (2016). *Build Nigeria: Tackling the construction skills gap through entrepreneurship*. E-paper.

Thompson, J. F. (2002). *Foundation of Vocational Education*. New York: Practice Hall-Inc.

Tolu, L. and Abe, O. (2011). *National Development in Nigeria: issues challenges and prospects*. Journal of Public Administration and Policy Research. *3*(9). 237-341.

Winner, R. K. (2002). *Rung by rung up the health career ladder. American Vocational Journal*. 48 (7): 18-27.

excellent4omo@gmail.com

CHAPTER 9

SCALING UP RURAL YOUTH PARTICIPATION IN AGRIPRENEURSHIP: A STRATEGY TO NATIONAL DEVELOPMENT

Innocent ABALI (PhD)
Department of Agricultural Education, Federal College of Education (Technical), Omoku, Rivers State, Nigeria.

Abstract

African countries, Nigeria inclusive have a huge youth population in rural areas where agriculture is mostly practiced. This important part of the demography is facing high rates of unemployment, underemployment and poverty. The scaling up of rural youths involvement in agripreneurship has the potential of providing the employment opportunities, improving the livelihood of youth-agripreneurs, turning around the rural economy and engendering national development. The paper recommends the scaling up of rural youth involvement in agripreneurship for self and national development by governments and concerned private sector interests.

Keywords: Agripreneur, Agripreneurship, Rural Youth, National development

Introduction

A gripreneurship refers to agricultural entrepreneurship, which is an important factor in the economic evolution of agrarian and emerging nations. The concept of agricultural entrepreneurship (agripreneurship) focuses attention on enhancing production methods and expanding market opportunities. An agripreneur is a business owner whose primary focus is agriculture or agriculture-related activities. Consistency, innovative thinking, risk taking, communication, and in general, application of good management approaches are skills that a successful agripreneurs must possess. Farmers require knowledge in aspects such as planning, implementing and controlling of farm management and also agricultural techniques and methods like production, harvesting, processing into finished goods, wholesaling and retailing, financial management, and accessing storage and transport, promotion, and advisory services.

Concept Of Youth

The concept of youth is defined differently by different people. The United Nations and the International Labour Organization define youth in terms of age bracket. Youths fall into the age bracket 15 and 24 years. The African Union considers those between the ages of 15 and 35 to be young. Even within Sub Sahara African the age range varies from 15 to 30 years old in Kenya, 18 to 35 years in Nigeria, and 15 to 40 years old in Mali (FGN, 2009; Filmer and Fox, 2014). Often, the end purpose of the measurement determines the demarcation (Proctor and Lucchesi, 2012).

In Nigeria, graduates over 30 years old are not eligible for the National Youth Service Corps (NYSC) system although persons 35 years old are deemed youth under national policy. Youth are a diverse group (FGN, 2009), just as the overall community from which they emerge. Nigeria's National Youth Policy recognizes youth as the country's most important and valuable resource. As a result, the government needs to "recognize, discover, and comprehend their conditions, requirements, interests, issues, ambitions, ideas, and capacities, and create suitable provisions for their growth and development" (FGN, 2009). The policy also notes that "youth are the most active, volatile, and yet most susceptible elements of the population" (FGN, 2009). Young women, disabled youths, those living in rural areas and urban slums, and the unemployed are among the priority targets and vulnerable youngsters (Moore, 2015).

Youth deserve realistic economic options not only to meet their immediate financial requirements and those of their families but also to ensure their long-term well-being. Young people can develop financial assets, competencies, social networks, sustainable livelihoods, and overall social and economic well-being by taking advantage of opportunities (Moore, 2015). In the case of Nigerian youths, these chances can be found in the form of agripreneurship in the agribusiness where large scale commercialization of production is important (Maillu, Mukulu, and Kahiri, 2016).

Cases Of Agripreneurship In Africa

Agricultural entrepreneurship is known as agripreneurship. The Global Forum for Rural Advisory Services (GFRAS) describes it as an "adaptive and dynamic process of agricultural business growth that delivers innovation and value addition, accelerates value creation, and allows for sustainable systems that enable equitable social impact" (Ferris, Chander, and Ernst, 2017). It refers to agricultural business activities that are long-term, market-driven, and socially responsible at all levels of operation (Uneze, 2013). Agripreneurship can assist rural youths become more effective actors in the *agrifood* value chain by providing new work possibilities and sources of empowerment in addition to increasing their livelihood options.

Agripreneurs provide value at both the upstream and downstream ends of the agricultural value chain (Losch, 2016). Farmers, traders, processors, retailers, and business service providers such as agro-input dealers, production services, equipment maintenance services, market intelligence services, and financial service providers are examples of those who help to facilitate the value chain (Ferris et al., 2017; Proctor and Lucchesi, 2012). Horticulture, arable farming, aquaculture, forestry, and cattle are agricultural and rural economic subsectors where youths can be found (Emerhirhi et al., 2017; IITA, 2014; Maillu et al., 2016; Sanginga, 2015; Uneze, 2013). As a result, agribusiness opportunities for small and medium companies (SMEs) abound at every level of the value chain. Agriculture is not only the largest employer of labor in rural community, but also has the potential to spur regional economic growth and provide much-needed jobs for youths (Filmer and Fox, 2014).

In developing countries, the youth-agripreneur nexus is not always bleak. There have been some initiatives that have been successful. In 2012, the International Institute for Tropical Agriculture (IITA) in Ibadan, Nigeria, launched its young agripreneurship program (IYA). The initiative was successful in influencing youngsters' attitudes toward agribusiness (IITA, 2014; Sanginga, 2015). It was dynamic in terms of youth training and retraining, as well as its use of social media platforms for extensive communication and mobilization and value addition (IITA, 2014). The initiative was so successful that it was reproduced in the Democratic Republic of Congo in 2013, Tanzania in 2014, Kenya in 2015, and Uganda in 2016.

In 2013 and 2014, the Federal Government of Nigeria (FGN) collaborated with FAO to launch the Youth Employment in Agriculture Program (YEAP) and the Youth and Women in Agribusiness Investment Program (YWAIP), both of which were successful (Adesugba and Mavrotas, 2016a). Red Fox Ethiopia is a large horticulture company run by German businessmen. It provides about 1,300 jobs especially to young people and women. Another example is vegetable production in Madagascar, where tens of thousands of small-scale farmers work together (Filmer and Fox, 2014).

Areas Of Agripreneurship Development

Some of the areas where agripreneurship can be developed in emerging economies include but are not limited to:

- Honey Production

Beekeeping and honey production provide youths with a plethora of untapped prospects.

- Plant Clinics

Farmers face difficulties in identifying and treating weeds, illnesses, microbial attacks, and crop pests. Plant clinics can be set up by agriculture graduates to combat these issues.

- Landscaping and Nursery

The need for greener environments has been steadily increasing. However, there is a demand-supply mismatch, as well as the issue of accessibility. By filling this void, the nursery sector has offered an opportunity for many. The growing sector of corporate and commercial landscaping is worth noting.

- Food Processing

Small and medium-sized businesses can start projects such as finger-chip plants, potato-chip plants, tomato-sauce plants, and so on.

- Mineral Water with a Herbal Base

The herbal industry is prospering in Nigeria as a result of the ongoing campaigns against chemical risks. The discovery of significant levels of pesticides in beverages and related issues have bolstered the argument that herbs are safe. For aspiring agripreneurs, this industry is a gold mine.

- Animal Supplements

Although there is a demand-supply mismatch in animal feed due to high cost of inputs, small-scale plants can be built up to meet current demands.

- Medicinal Plant Cultivation

Because of the growing demand for herbal medicines and the tendency of pharmaceutical corporations to manufacture such medications, medicinal plant cultivation offers strong agribusiness potential. The production of these medicines will necessitate raw materials in the form of medicinal plant products, which agripreneurs can supply.

- Extension of Cyberspace

Farmers' interest in using the internet to understand soil conditions, crop protection tips, weather forecasts, and other topics have been neglected in rural areas. The need to raise enthusiasm for the internet to facilitate understanding of soil conditions, crop protection tips, weather forecasts, and other topics become imperative. Agripreneurial extension combined with rural customized strategy is a desirable option.

- Floriculture Promotion

Floriculture marketing has good potentials as agribusiness venture. The options are many and include floral shops, wholesale trading, electronic retailing, and so forth.

- Development of Poultry and Fisheries

The consumption of meat and eggs has been steadily increasing. This has given aspiring poultry entrepreneurs a chance to start their own firms. Poultry farming facilitates diversification for operators in crop production or as businesses on their own.

- Fishery

The fishing industry has provided significant opportunities in both the home and export markets. Agribusiness efforts in this approach can be extremely beneficial.

- Farm Machinery

Customized farm machinery and equipment are in demand. Traditional farm machinery for instance do not work in steep areas due to the topography. Agricultural engineers can build small but handy and strong farm machinery and tools to meet local needs.

Other agripreneurial areas include:

- Dairy
- Insurance

- Agri-eco tourism
- Research and development
- Pesticide production and marketing
- Bio-fertilizer production and marketing
- Seed processing and agribusiness
- Veterinary clinics
- Soil testing laboratory
- Post-harvest management
- Vegetable production and marketing
- Organic production/food chain
- Direct and retail marketing
- Contract farming

Concept Of National Development Agripreneurship

The term "national development" encompasses a wide range of activities in the life of a nation using a holistic approach. It sometimes involves a process of reconstruction and development in numerous aspects of a nation and by extension, individuals that make up the nation. Industries, agriculture, education, social, religious, and cultural organizations all need to flourish and expand to their full potentials for the term national development to fully apply. It is best defined as the holistic and balanced development of a nation's various features and facets, including political, economic, social, cultural, scientific, and material.

National development as noted by the United Nations Decade Report, is best defined as growth plus change. Change includes the social, cultural, and economic aspects in qualitative and quantitative terms.

In general, national development encompasses the following parameters:
i) development through a planned national economy

(ii) increase in agricultural production through application of modern technical know-how

(iii) harnessing industrial production

(iv) human resource development, and

(v) application of science and technology in the production sector.

Traditionally, agriculture is viewed as a way of life especially in the non-industrialized continents of Africa and Asia. The importance of an entrepreneurial culture in the agricultural sector has however been recognized in recent decades. Through the development of entrepreneurial and organizational competency, farmers work in an organized manner and develop sustainable competitive advantage which has facilitated successful competition in regional, national, and international markets. Also, sustainable development of agricultural land depends on the development of organizational and entrepreneurial competencies in farmers.

Therefore agripreneurship is a call to make agriculture attractive and profitable business engagement thereby promoting national development. Agriculture possesses a wide scope for entrepreneurship which can be harnessed by effective management of agri-elements such as water, seed, soil, and market situations.

Writing on agricultural innovative systems the World Bank (2012) observes that agriculture and domestic businesses provide about 50% of employment in developing countries but fails to produce sufficient income to raise people out of poverty. Consequently, entrepreneurial actions associated with agriculture create solution for growing household income. With good managerial skills in rural youths and entrepreneurial expertise supported by government measures, the growing needs of agribusiness can be facilitated thereby contributing to national development.

Agripreneurship contributes to national income and direct employment especially in rural areas. Value-added products provide entrepreneurs with larger return on investments and profits. Thus, agripreneurs have to take advantage of change in consumer demand and satisfy consumers' needs.

Agripreneurship can also support social and economic development, reduction in poverty index, and ensure good nutrition and food security. In addition, it can foster diversification of the economy and income bases by providing employment and entrepreneurial opportunities for rural youths thereby contributing immensely to national development.

Needs For Scaling Up Rural Youth Participation In Agripreneurship

Scaling up is discussed hereunder under several sub-headings:

Leadership - Scaling up, in the opinion of Hatmann and Linn (2008) necessitates political and organizational leadership, vision, and values, if rural youth-agripreneurs do not lead the scaling-up process with a clear vision, if agripreneurs do not embody clear set of values that empower managers and staff to continuously challenge themselves, and if individuals within institutions are not given the incentives to push themselves and others to scale up successful interventions, the current pattern of pervasive "short-termism" and fragmentation of effort will continue to characterize agribusiness. The view of Hatmann and Linn was supported by USAID (2014) which holds that the key ingredients for successful scaling up of agripreneurship for national development include the vision of the ultimate scale at which the innovation (agripreneurship) will be judged to be successful. The following elements must be present for an innovation (agripreneurship) to be considered scalable (WHO, 2010):

* Trustworthiness (if the innovation has sound evidence or proven advocates)

* Pertinence (if the innovation adequately addresses problems at hand)

* Benefits (if the innovation is advantageous over other alternatives)

* Appropriateness is one of the most important factors to consider (if the innovation fits the needs and context of the user).

Technology - For adoption to be effective, simplicity in execution must be prioritized. In other words, the technology or invention should be as simple to deploy as possible. Before releasing a technology or invention for scaling up, thorough validation process is critical.

Pathways for scaling up – These have to be identified because there are several options for expanding a successful agribusiness. According to IFAD (2010) a "route" is an understanding of the actions that must be performed in the innovation learning-scaling up cycle to ensure that a successful pilot is moved from its experimental stage to the scale eventually determined to be appropriate for the desired degree of impact. To realize the vision, key actors must explore and implement scaling up pathways to include bringing a known technology to agripreneurs, testing its introduction at the local level, evaluating the impact and adoption process, and moving forward with replication and adaptation based on the lessons learned (USAID, 2014).

Effective partnerships - Some writers have emphasized good collaboration as a key aspect in scaling up innovation particularly in agribusiness. This is because a coordinating platform for strategic collaboration among key stakeholders is required. Key partners in scaling up as noted by Jonasova and Cooke (2012) should always be mobilized and used.

Partnerships are critical especially in reaching out to end users. The importance of determining whether domestic or external partners would continue or step up to support agripreneurship has been found to have a vital influence in scaling up intervention. As a result, Mansuri and Rao (2004) observe that in majority of successful scaling up activities, partners were a critical factor.

Enabling Environment - Building effective extension systems, policy reform, expanding access to credit and financing, conserving natural resources, accounting for social, cultural, and political realities on the ground, and building local cooperation and partnerships are all examples of creating the space or to foster the right conditions for scaling up.

Scaling efforts in innovative practices like agripreneurship as posited by Jonasova and Cooke (2012) require enabling settings to grow thus:

i.   Policy

Studies have shown that scaling up agripreneurship ideas requires legislative, regulatory, and legal framework. Scaling up initiatives are frequently hampered by policy difficulties particularly in value chain growth. Price controls, onerous regulatory requirements, and subsidies targeted at specific market participants as well as monopolies in processing or trading can function as disincentives. To facilitate scaling up activities, policy and legal frameworks in the focus nations must be enacted.

Hatmann and Linn (2008) also argue that the policy framework, laws, regulations, and conventions must be beneficial if scaling up is to be effective. USAID (2014) holds that the policy environment can either constrain or accelerate the scale up of productive innovations or businesses. Laws, treatises, regulations, pronouncements, administrative acts, and financial priorities are examples of policy. Scaling activities are influenced by policy approaches, implementation procedures, and activities that direct government actions and enforcement. Hatmann and Linn (2008) argue that the policy framework, laws, regulations, and conventions must be beneficial if scaling up is to be effective.

ii.   Markets

Potential market limits must be identified and handled when scaling up agricultural products to avoid negative price consequences (IIRR, 2000) market development.

iii.   Institutional capacities

Institutional and organizational capacities should be adequate and personnel should possess the necessary skills.

iv.   Culture and gender

Potential cultural or gender barriers should always be addressed and changes should be made to allow for scaling up. Potential cultural barriers or support mechanisms must be recognized and the intervention need be appropriately tailored to allow scale in a culturally varied context (USAID, 2014).

The United Nations Food and Agriculture Organization (FAO, 2009) emphasizes advocacy in scaling up agricultural innovations. Political outreach, constituency building, and pro-active advocacy are all necessary, as are lobbying to influence policymakers, training public officials, media mobilization, and networking through professional and political channels. Kohl (2007) opines that to expand and sustain agripreneurship, political support need be gained early in the process through lobbying techniques.

Capacity building - Training and development of staff in charge of scaling up initiatives is important although not a panacea in and of itself because training in agripreneurship development will not have a lasting impact without the other key elements of institutional capacity building such as leadership, political support, incentives, and so on. It has been reported that lack of properly trained human resources is frequently a major stumbling block to scaling up. As a result, quality training in conjunction with appropriate incentives is recommended as a critical component of scaling up. The purpose of the pilot phase is to build an effective and efficient program design but if the lessons learnt are not consistently utilized, the effort may be squandered. Training aids in the transmission of procedural and technical competence as well as organizational ideals to new hires ensure that this is important otherwise intangible assets are not diminished as the company grows.

Existing employees require training to support their continued professional development as the agribusiness grows and new issues emerge. Binswanger and Nguyen (2005) stress the importance of training when it comes to scaling up community-driven development programs. Binswanger and Aiyar (2003) focus on the development of manuals to aid in the implementation of agripreneurship expansion. Kohl (2007) however notes that training should not be seen as the universal response to capacity gaps while overlooking the importance of other critical success factors such as the creation of adequate incentives and accountabilities.

Scaling up needs incentives and accountability - Innovation may be hampered and the scaling-up process may fail if appropriate incentives are not in place. Incentives for key actors must be included in scaling up processes. These can be positive rewards for achieving scaling up goals or penalties for failing to achieve them. They can be monetary or non-monetary (recognition and status, also promotion or election to office and hence influence). One important tool for creating incentives is to plan for incremental steps with early results rather than building the perfect programme to be rolled out after a long preparation time without intermediate results (Hatmann and Linn (2008).

Recommendations

The following recommendations are made:
i. The scaling-up process of rural youth involvement in agripreneurship should have a clear vision and values that empower all the stakeholders especially at the grassroots level to continuously challenge themselves to scale up.
ii. Government should create an enabling environment for scaling up rural youth involvement in agripreneurship
iii. The risk of utilizing scaling up processes in agripreneurship to gain political benefit should be avoided
iv. Capacity building and training in agripreneur-

ship development among rural youths should be encouraged by the major stakeholders.

Conclusion

Scaling up rural youth involvement in agripreneurship can assist rural youths to become more effective actors in the *agrifood* value chain by giving new work possibilities and sources of empowerment. It can also increase their livelihood options thereby contributing to national development.

References

Binswanger H. P., & Aiyar, S. S. (2013). Scaling up community-driven development: Theoretical underpinnings and programme design implications. Washibgton DC: The World Bank. (World Bank Policy Research Working Paper No. 3039). Retrieved, December 20, 2021 from http://pubs.iied.org

Emerhirhi, E., Nnadi, F. N., Chikaire, J. U., Anyoha, N. ., & Ejiogu-Okereke, N. (2017). Rural women agri-preneurship opportunities for poverty reduction and improved livelihood in Imo State, Nigeria. *Journal of Dynamics in Agricultural Research*, 4(2), 16–23.

Food & Agricultural Organization. (2009). Scaling up conservation agriculture in Africa: Strategy and approaches. Rome: FAO.

Ferris, S., Chander, M., & Ernst, N. (2017). *Rural advisory services for agripreneurship development.* (GFRAS Global good practice notes for extension and advisory services No. 30) (Vol. 12). Lindau,

Federal Republic of Nigeria. (2009). Second national youth policy. Retrieved, December 01, 2021 from http://nigeria.unfpa.org/pdf/snyp2009.pdf

Filmer, D., & Fox, L. (2014). *Youth employment in Sub-Saharan Africa*. Washington, DC:

Hatmann, A., & Linn, J.F. (2008). Scaling up: A framework and lessons for development effectiveness from literature and practice. Wolfensolin Centre for Development Working Paper 5.

International Fund for Agricultural Development. (2010). IFAD's strategic framework 2007-2010: A summary. Retrieved, November 09, 2021 from http://www.ifad.org/sf/.

International Institute for Tropical Agriculture. (2014). *Moving forward: IITA annual report.*

International Institute of Rural Reconstruction. (2000). Going to scale: Can we bring more benefits to more people more quickly? Conference highlights April 10-14. Philippines: IIRR

Jonasova, M., & Cooke S. (2012). Thinking systematically about scaling up World Bank supported agriculture and rural development operations: The case of competitive grant schemes for agricultural research and extension. World Bank Discussion Paper 53. Washington, DC: The World Bank.

Kohl, R. (2007). Key points for scaling up management systems international. Power Point Presentation to the Wolfensohn Center.

Losch, B. (2016). Structural transformation to boost youth labour demand in sub-Saharan Africa: The role of agriculture, rural areas and territorial development (No. 204). Employment Policy Department Working Paper. Retrieved November 02 from http://agritrop.cirad.fr/582221/

Maillu, J., Mukulu, E., & Kahiri, J. (2016). Credit from group savings associations and the *change*. London. Retrieved from http://pubs.iied.org

Moore, K. (2015). Fostering economic opportunities for youth in Africa: A comprehensive approach. *Enterprise Development and Microfinance*. 26 (2). 195–209. http://doi.org/10.3362/1755-1986.2015.017 Performance of Smallholder Horticultural Agripreneurs in Kenya. *International Journal of Economics, Commerce, and Management.* 4(12). 549–563. Retrieved from http://ijecm.co.uk/

Proctor, F. J., & Lucchesi, V. (2012). Small-scale farming and youth in an era of change. Retrieved, January 10, 2021 from www.researchgate.net>publications>265672547_Small-scale_Farming-and-youth-in-an-era-of-change

Saliu, O. J., Onuche, U., & Abubakar, H. (2016). Perception of Kogi State university agricultural students on farming as career. *International Journal of Sustainable Agricultural Research. 3* (4). 72–81. http://doi.org/10.18488/journal.70/2016.3.4/70.4.72.8

Sanginga, N. (2015). *Youth in agribusiness within an African agricultural transformation agenda. Feeding Africa.* Retrieved from https://www.afdb.org/fileadmin/uploads/af db/Documents/Events/DakAgri2015/Youth_in_Agribusiness_within_an_African_Agricultural_Transformation_Agenda.pdf

The World Bank. (2012). Agricultural innovation systems: An investment sourcebook. World Bank. Retrieved, December 20, 2021 from http://doi.org/http://dx.doi.org/10.1596/978-1-4648-0107-5

Uneze, C. (2013). Adopting agripreneurship education for Nigeria's quest for food security in Vision 20:2020. *Greener Journal of Educational Research (GJER), 3*(9), 1–8. Retrieved from http://gjournals.org/GJER/GJER PDF/2013/November/180913848 Uneze.pdf%0Ahttp://www.global-academi cgroup.com/journals/pristine/ADOPTING AGRIPRENEURSHIP EDUCATION FOR NIGERIA.pdf

United States Aid for International Development. (2014). Scaling up the adoption and use of agricultural technologies. Global learning and evidence exchange (GLEE). Bangkok, Thailand. January 7-9 2014.

World Health Organization. (2010). Nine steps for developing a scaling up strategy." Geneva: World Health Organisation.

Retrieved October 20, 2021 from http://whqlibdoc.who.int publications/2010/9789241500319_eng. pdf? Ua =1.

abaliinnocent@gmail.com

PHILOSOPHICAL ISSUES FOR DEVELOPMENT
OF NIGERIA AND AFRICA

CHAPTER 10

SCIENCE, TECHNOLOGICAL DEVEL-
OPMENT, AND HUMAN VALUES

Professor Joseph Donatus OKOH
Former Deputy Vice Chancellor
University of Port Harcourt
Nigeria

Introduction

We live in a world that is pierced through and through by science and technology. No nation can pretend to be indifferent to the tremendous power for good and for evil of science and technology. This is true because many of the major economic, political, social, and personal decisions for both the developed and the developing nations depend upon a clear, rational understanding of the potentials and directions of science and technology for national development. Science, in the opinion of Hard (1975) describes the world as it is, while technology remakes the world to serve human desires. Service to man and society is thus the primary function of science and technology. The Nigerian National Policy on Education (FRN, 2014) recognizes this service role, when in enumerating the aims of technical education it states: "to provide people who can apply scientific knowledge to the improvement and solution of environmental problems for the use and convenience of man".

It is however a drama of profound tragedy that the lofty ideal of science and technology for the service of man and society is evermore being debilitated by the intrusion of politics, prejudice, self-interest and unethical means and ends. Instead of protecting and promoting the three basic human values of "the beautiful the good and the true" There seem to be a strange contradiction between an increase in scientific and technological knowledge and the pursuit of human values. We seem to be faced with two unpalatable alternatives: either discourage and dismantle modern science and technology or face a likely destruction of human values, human society and the environment. Is this science versus ethical human development dilemma real?

In this brief essay we wish to show that first, the dilemma in question is not caused by anything in the nature of science and technology. Secondly, we wish to show that what creates the dilemma is the anti-social attitude and the politics of those who control science, and technological development.

Ethical Basis Of Science And Technology

Many scientists and technocrats have felt and continue to feel that the realm of ethics is the exclusive preserve of the philosophers and the humanists. Hence, they have abdicated any interest in the ethical implications of their inventions and products. On the other hand, some philosophers and humanists have not only treated these scientists with contempt, they have often insisted that the scientists alone are to blame for the ills of modern science and technology. It is true that no philosopher has ever made a nuclear weapon or created radioactive waste. Yet he cannot wash his hands of blame, because we live in a world whose ills grow more often from inaction than from error.

Instead of helping to educate the scientist to appreciate the ethical basis of science and technology, the philosopher has tended to disdain science and to wash his hands off the ills of technological development. This attitude helps no one. As Bronowski (1965) aptly points out, "there is no more threatening and no more degrading doctrine than the fancy that somehow we may shelve the responsibility for making the decisions of our society by passing it to a few scientists armored with a special magic" (p. 5). The world today is made it is powered by science. The philosopher must accept this fact. And inconsequence of it, he must work relentlessly to see that those who build and who will be building our bridges, canning our food, manufacturing our medicine, and so on, are made to realize the ethical consequences of science and technology. The philosopher must help the scientist to reflect a sensitivity to human values.

Science and technology cannot be divorced from ethics. At the very heart of every scientific discovery there ought to be an ethical conception. This would mean that the supreme test of all scientific and industrial development must be based on the contribution they make to the all-round healthy growth of every member of society. Hard highlights the essential role of value in science and technological when he says that although science provides knowledge and technology provides ways of using this knowledge, it is nevertheless our value concepts which guide what we ought to do with science and technology (Brownosky, 1965).

Science as a body of knowledge designed to "perfect the habit of truth", uplift "the imaginative acts of human understanding and creativity" and bring about the sense of "human dignity" is indeed based on an ethical conception (Dewey, 2000). This includes (a) conceptions of the meaning of life (b) conceptions of the type of society worth attaining and (c) an envisaged idea of what constitutes right and wrong. Under such headings the scientist/technologist would be asking questions like these:

a)   Is scientific knowledge for personal self-perfection, self-realization in the community, or is it only for efficiency in industrial production?

b)   Can the scientist's personal interest, override the general well-being of the community?

c)   Must inventions be directed by social needs or personal/ co-operate interests?

d)   Can anything be called a scientific discovery which neither makes life more orderly nor give unity and cohesion to the common experience of man?

Basic to John Dewey's reconstruction in philosophy, is the conception of logical continuity "between the material, the mechanical, the scientific and the moral" (Dewey, 1957). Dewey not only rejected but also lamented the existing apparent conflict between science and morals. He is dissatisfied over "the intellectual scandal that seemed to be involved in the current (and traditional) dualism in logical standpoint and method between something called "science" on the one hand and something called "morals" on the other" (Dewey, 2000).

The point that is being made in this section of the essay is that the very nature of science precludes any question of there being the dilemma of science versus ethics within the area of national development. By its nature science is based on the pursuit of "the beautiful, the good and the truth". How then does the dilemma of science versus human values arise?

As science and technology developed first in Western World and then in the Eastern bloc, these societies had to carefully work-out certain human values that ought to guide the activity of scientific and technological development.

In Western Europe and North America, we have had, beginning from the early 18th century the concept of Self-interest, then came Enlighten Self-interest, then the Utilitarian principle of the greatest happiness of the greatest number; this was followed by the labour-theory of value which is the off-shoot of capitalism.

In the East, Marxism emerged as a reaction to the socio-economic policy of a laissez-faire Capitalist social order. Marxism teaches, in a paraphrase of Amare (1982) that man's various modes of consciousness, his morality, art, science, and technological development are products of his material conditions and reflected in his class interests. Human history, according to Marxism, is propelled forward by the power that issues from class struggle and leads to an inevitable destination a classless social order.

Because of their respective political and ideological positions, there are broad differences in the role and use of science and technology in the Liberal-Capitalist society and in the Marxist society. The Liberal Capitalists assume that once science has progressed so that we know how to achieve a given result technically, the problem then becomes one of convincing policy-makers that the solution should be put into operation (Amare, 1982). Very often, the only concern is the profit and loss equation. Liberal-capitalist society is basically one which accepts the structure of power and privilege, as such it sees the problem of science versus ethics as one of the "dangers of technology" and its effects.

Marxists on the other hand, have a completely different approach. According to the Marxist view, the ethical implications of the uses of new scientific knowledge can only be judged according to which of the two classes – owners of the means of production who run their businesses primarily to -make a profit, and workers who sell their labour in order just to make a living – will primarily benefit from it.

Three simple rule-of-thumb, as opined by Chasim (1974) guide Marxists in analyzing how science will be utilized in capitalist society:

1.   Advances which improve the lives of workers will only be acceptable to the owners of the means of production if they also happen to serve the interests of the latter;
2.   When there is an advance beneficial only to workers, the capitalists will make every attempt to evade or prevent its implementation (for example, mass transit);
3.   An advance profitable to the capitalists which happens to bring great harm to workers, will be used by the capitalists as long as they can manage to do so (for example, pesticides, chemicals in foods).

The Marxist therefore concludes that the apparent science-ethics dilemma will disappear only in a classless society in which science would come under the control of the masses. Any discovery which would harm most people could not be put to use simply because it would bring profits to a few.

Science And Technology: The Nigerian Scene

Science and technology have become the gateway toward modernization. Black (1966) has defined modernization as "the process by which historically evolved institutions are adapted to the rapidly changing functions that reflect the unprecedented increase in man's knowledge, permitting control over his environment, that accompanied the scientific revolution" (p. 7). In the world of today, no nation has the privilege of standing aloof from either the process or the problems of modernization. As Levy (1966) puts it, "We may not like greater modernization, we may love it, we may be neutral about it, but it is nevertheless going to be terribly important to each of us" (p. 31).

Nigeria is a nation grappling with the staggering problems of seeking to become modernized yet faced with the mountainous forces of how to adapt the present to her traditional past. Part of the present moral and intellectual malaise in Nigeria today can be blamed on the random character which the process of modernization has been allowed to assume. It has undermined all basis of traditional human values and the criteria for identifying what excellencies are worth pursuing.

A people's way of life ought to grow in the same proportion as her scientific and industrial development. In other words, the stages of moral and intellectual maturity ought to match the general stages of a country's modernization process itself. We have already, elsewhere in this essay, referred to how Europe, beginning from the dawn of the Scientific Revolution had to slowly but steadily work-out certain human values that guided the process of modernization which Europeans were then undergoing. Unfortunately, we have a situation in Nigeria where the stages of the process of modernization has totally out-stripped the development of human values.

Unlike his Western or Eastern counterpart, the Nigerian scientist lacks a commitment to a viable ethical and/or ideological base. He is not at home with his African traditional values. At the same time, he has to undergo frequent mental torture while trying to decide whether to adapt either the Capitalist or the Marxist concept of the use of science and technology. In his pursuit of modernization, many a Nigerian scientist/technocrat has exhibited unethical attitudes which are the reflections of an even deeper malaise, namely, the lack of values to live by. This has manifested itself in such forms as forgery and the exploitation of fellow citizens.

While we do not wish to exonerate other Nigerian professional groups from any blame, our special focus here is on the scientists, technologists, and industrialist. If the argument we established in part two of this essay is accepted we are forced to conclude that the catalogue of industrial woes mentioned below, portray the role of science and technology in Nigeria as being partisan and overtly profit oriented. There are fake umbilical cord nets; fake rice and fake products of all types in our markets.

Someone may protest and say all of the above indictments could only be rightly directed at the petty manufacturer. So, let us go a step further and look at the oil industry in Nigeria. We admit that we cannot produce crude oil without some gas coming along with it. But according to experts there are three possible ways of controlling this gas: (1) harness and use the gas domestically and commercially; (2) re-inject the gas into the ground; (3) flare the gas. The Nigerian scientists- technologists have chosen to flare the gas, a measure which is harmful to the environment and innocent villagers who must inhale polluted air. As long as this cheap measure yields a whole lot of revenue for the government, who cares?

Akinyele (1983) in a paper titled "Twenty-five years of Engineering in Nigeria" chided Nigerian engineers for poor qual-

163

ity jobs. Nigerian engineers, he said, placed less emphasis on practical job-related experience and often delegated "tough jobs" to semi-skilled men. This has resulted in poor quality of engineering services and a breakdown in confidence of policy-makers in the ability of Nigerian engineers and the resultant vicious circle of foreign dependence. Commenting on the false values of Nigerian medical scientists, Bashua (1983) has this to say:

> Our experts and scientists should readily admit their lacklustre performance and their failure to pursue purposeful advanced medical and allied development strategies. Their unpatriotic attitude of preferring imported materials to developing local stuff which could foster a sense of belonging; of merely dispensing drugs and allied products instead of mobilizing resources to produce their own products, is responsible in part for the drugs, food and other problems which are purely symptomatic of a larger malaise.

Science deals with human problems and tries to find solutions to them. The Nigerian scientist/technologist is not yet fully educated about the ethical basis of science and technology. The manufacturer who makes and sells fake baby food, fake medicine and so on, cannot claim to be either a scientist or a technologist. We strongly suggest that at this stage of our national development every effort must be made to include ethics in the curriculum of all Nigerian institutions where science is taught.

Conclusion

From the analysis of the fore going problem we have been able to establish first, the necessity of the philosophers and the scientists to work-hand-in-hand to destroy the myth of science versus ethics. If our scientists and technologists do not operate from prejudice and, self-interest or adopt partisan mode of thought and action, the world could be spared the agony of underdevelopment and irreparable damage to human kind.

The challenge to the Nigerian scientists and technologists is for them to work in collaboration with other scholars from Africa to evolve authentic indigenous values which ought to guide the development of science and technology in Africa. In the absence of such indigenous values, African scientists must learn to strike a balance between the excesses of a laissez-faire Capitalist attitude to science and technology on the hand, and the Marxist attitude, on the other.

References

Hard, P. D. (1975). Science, technology, and society: New goals for interdisciplinary science teaching. *The Science Teacher*. 27; 30.

Federal Republic of Nigeria (2014). *National policy on education*. Lagos: NERDC Press.

Schlick, M. (1927). The original, Vom Sinn Des Lebens, On the Meaning of Life (David Rynin).

Bronowski, J. (1965). *Science and human values*. London: Harper & Row.

Dewey, J. (1957). *Reconstruction in philosophy*. Boston: The Beacon Press. p. 173.

Dewey. J. (2000). Science and the future of society. In J. Partner. Intelligence in the modern world. New York: The Modern Library.

Amare, G. (1982). *Nigerian Journal of Educational Philosophy*. 1 (1). 9.

Chasim, B., & Chasiri, G. (1974). *Power and politics: A Marxist approach to political sociology*.

Black, C. E. (1966). The dynamics of modernization: A study in comparative history. New York: Harper and Row.

Levy Jr., M. J. (1966). Modernization and the structure of societies. Princeton, New Jersey:
        Princeton University Press. Vol. 1. p. 31.

Akinyele, T. (1983, December 08). *The Guardian*. Vol. 1, No. 176.

Bashua, F. A. (1983, December 15). *The Guardian*. VoI. 1, No. 23, p 9.

jdokoh@yahoo.com

CHAPTER 11

THE PHILOSOPHY OF JUSTICE AND NATIONAL DEVELOPMENT

Ibitamuno Mitchell AMINIGO
Fulbright Scholar & Professor of Philosophy of Education
Faculty of Education, University of Port Harcourt, Port Harcourt

Introduction

For the past one hundred years Africa has lived through a lot of crises which began with the advent of colonialism. The original political units and social formations were made to give way to modern polities modeled on the principles of western democracy. Yet the people have not been able to overcome the confusion in the realm of values brought about by the clash of cultures which imperialism caused in Africa. People of diverse linguistic and cultural backgrounds were lumped together to live under the same administrative and political units. Under such circumstances the primordial values, loyalties and affinities could not meaningfully cope with the challenges of political existence in nation states. The result has been a lot of political strife and social injustice as witnessed in Ethiopia, Sudan, Somalia, Nigeria, Chad, Liberia, the Democratic Republic of Congo and many other parts of the continent where nation-building has meant a lot of social stress.

In the Nigerian experience it took a thirty-month civil war (1967-1970) before the second National Development Plan (1970-1974) was drawn up to give a clear picture of the kind of society that was desired. The emergent statement of national objectives is an eloquent testimony of the people's desire to transform the crisis-torn polity into a more humane, just, and democratic society. As a nation Nigeria now aims to build:

1. a free and democratic society
2. a just and egalitarian society
3. a united, strong, and self-reliant nation
4. a great and dynamic economy
5. a land of bright and full opportunities for all citizens.
   (FRN, 2014)

A close examination of the afore-stated national objectives indicates that one major area of need is an understanding of, and commitment to human values of justice. This is because justice is the primary social construct that makes for peace, order, and freedom in any human society. A measure of realization of this fact led to the Federal Government programme tagged MAMSER (Mass Mobilization for Self-Reliance, Social Justice, and Economic Recovery) launched on 25th July 1987. This was a crusade in the late 1980's charged with the task of formulating a programme of political education geared towards enlightening the generality of Nigerians on the need for a democratic society and the enthronement of social justice which would lead to the economic recovery the nation needs very urgently. Indeed Gana (1989) then Chairman of the MAMSER Directorate had declared, "We must struggle to build a just and egalitarian society in Nigeria within the framework of freedom, democracy, and social justice" (p.13).

The statement above which anchors on the need for social and moral principles and values as the bases for ideas on the physical and economic aspects of national development should be seen as an imperative. This writer reasons that the question of justice is central in this regard. Indeed, the values of effective and patriotic citizenship, good neighbourliness, national consciousness, and better human relationships cannot be meaningful outside the context of the concept of justice. A good understanding of justice values will give us Africans the key to the ethical requirements of the national development process on the continent. It is therefore, easy to see that with the related concepts of human rights, democracy, freedom, liberty, equality, and fairness, a vigorous conceptualization of justice as a cardinal social value is a *sine qua non* for the attainment of national objectives in all African nations. This is because social life would then be conducive for individual and group existence, social, economic, and technological development.

The Philosopher's Task

It is in the light of the foregoing argument that the social, moral, and educational philosophers' task could be that of helping to clarify values requisite for social life. In the present enterprise this writer attempts to mirror the social challenges of our existential present in the Nigerian setting. This involves examining issues of justice, morality and education, ethnicity and many other social and topical issues that would help us articulate the values, concepts, and precepts that would enhance Nigeria's development as a nation. Such critical examination of social values would reveal the extent to which hunger, inequality, social injustice, group oppression, and other moral aberrations continue to scuttle plans for national development.

It is our proposition that national development efforts can better command general consent and appreciation in a social setting where the prime values of human rights and social justice have free course. For this reason, we contend that understanding of and commitment to values of justice as a sociopolitical construct would make it easier to direct the search for scientific and technological revolution to enhance social and economic development in Nigeria. If this happens, the revolution and development would then take place within the context of a just social order so that nobody or group of people would feel alienated or cheated in the scheme of things. This is because the overall quality of social life would then improve.

It is easy to see why justice needs to be enthroned in Nigeria and the rest of the African continent. In a lot of African countries there is cut-throat competition for scarce resources because of poverty that breeds rivalry. Secondly, colonialism brought together many ethnic groups into single political entities thereby promoting strife and group oppression. And because of ethnic loyalties it is difficult to forge political unity to enhance national development. Rather, we have the conflict generating questions of corruption, unfairness, uneven revenue allocation, unequal educational and employment opportunities, tribalism, political and cultural pluralism, tendencies that negate intra-national cohesion and progress. Thus, in Nigeria and most African countries, Bullivant (1980) posits that "The separate groups compete for economic, social, and political power. They regard each other suspiciously as threats to their own survival and their own well-being" (p.3).

In Nigeria if the situation is like this, national development would continue to be hindered and the quality of social life would remain poor. We therefore think that one way to enhance the quality of social life and relations is to ingrain justice and other moral values effectively into the education and other spheres of the body politic. This done, it becomes more feasible to work for the development of other resources in the nation. This is because a greater consciousness of justice would enhance social harmony since it is a value that is "trans-cultural, trans-religious, and trans-ethnic and can be appreciated by all citizens.

The Concept Of Justice

One major concern in philosophical thought over the years from Plato through Aristotle to the eighteenth-century thinkers such as Thomas Hobbes, John Locke, and Jean Jacques Rousseau up to contemporary ones such as John Rawls, J. R. Lucas and Ronald Dworkin has been the question of the social order of man's existence. Central to this enquiry about the ideal mode of man's existence is the problem of justice. In fact, Plato's concern in *The Republic* is the subject of justice, the essential social virtue that ought to determine human relationships and ensure the attainment of the good life for mankind. This search for justice has been the moving spirit of most discourse in moral philosophy, politics, jurisprudence, democratic movements, and economics. Indeed, Plato, we are told, was moved to explore the concept of justice better by constructing an ideal state in which justice would be fully manifest ('writ large'). The same concern for an ideal African society is what has motivated a lot of African writers and novelists. The explication of justice therefore is seen as a cardinal point in the present discourse. This essay shall be devoted to exploring some of the conceptions of justice so that its full implications for the African's search for an ideal society would be laid bare.

What Indeed Is Justice?

The concept of justice is the basic framework of social existence. Lucas (1980) believes 'justice is the bond of society' and quoting Hume, notes that no association of human individuals can subsist without it. This shows the importance of justice and the need for it to be not merely understood and appreciated in every society but seen to be at work in the relations and affairs of men. The individual can easily identify with the actions of a society or social set up because the actions and decisions have a rational basis which is founded on the moral principle of mutual consideration of each other's interest so that no man is done down unnecessarily.

Justice deals with fairness or propriety in the relationships of people with one another. Lucas (1980) equates justice with the uses of the words 'just' and 'fair' and their opposites 'unjust' and 'unfair'. From the contexts of usage, the word 'just' occurs more often in legal frameworks and the law courts, while the word 'fair' comes into use in contexts of games, families, and situations but the two words occasionally make inroads into each other in terms of usage. For instance, we may regard a court trial as fair or unfair and a school master or father as being just or unjust. If this argument is accepted, it becomes easy to see from usage that people, actions, decisions, laws, economic arrangements, legal procedures, games and social systems can be described as just or unjust. Lucas (1980) concludes by declaring that based on the usage of the words just and unjust,

> Justice is not the same as expediency, prudence, equality, liberty, generosity, friendliness, mercy or goodwill, and that since a decision can be said to be both just, in that it was reached by due process by an impartial judge who applied the relevant law, unjust in that the law itself was unjust or that the judge was precluded from taking certain relevant factors into consideration-justice itself must be a complicated concept (p.15).

The foregoing excerpt shows in clearly the reason justice is such a nebulous term although it is easily appreciated. It is used in contexts that suggest close resemblances with certain words, but its delineation depends on the soundness or efficiency of the arguments which lay it bare. But one fact is obvious and that is, since justice is a social construct, its significance comes into play when more than one party is involved in a matter. Hence the Greeks, according to Lucas (1980) thought of justice as 'the other chap's good.' Justice, from this perspective, does not arise if a man were an island unto himself; it is an "other-regarding" virtue. And therefore, it is the pivot of human relationships. When two or more people are involved in an enterprise of some sort, their relations can be regarded as just or unjust.

An act can only be regarded as just or unjust if it has bearing on the weal or woe of the person to whom it is done. Thus, justice has a distinct identity and is even better understood when examined from the negative angle. It is easy to see that injustice or unfairness arouses indignation and protest wherever it is seen at work. It is in fact difficult to imagine a warm embrace for anybody who is unfair in his dealings with others or an institution which is clearly seen to be unjust. The highlight of the above argument is that wherever justice is thwarted, or injustice is seen to reign, society cannot have the normal run or course of events going on. And the examination of the concept of justice above shows that institutional arrangements and socio-political and economic set ups can be subjected to the cold scrutiny of the concept of justice. This is an aspect of philosophical practice, and one key contribution of philosophy to national development.

Social Justice

With the concept of social justice, the meaning of justice goes beyond narrow application to the individual and is writ large to affect the larger society. As noted earlier, justice is seen as the criterion of social assessment and this means examining issues and practices of social arrangement and organization so that human happiness can be ensured, after all the institutions of society, whichever way they are arranged, affect people's fortunes, opportunities and attitudes to life. And the extent of concrete meaning this has for the citizens of any nation depends on the extent to which government is able to transform the ethical ideals of the social, political, and philosophical framework of each state, community or country. Thus, from the age of Plato, through Hobbes, Locke, Rousseau and John Stuart Mill to John Rawls, philosophers have grappled with the need to minimize social problems and conflicts by creating visions of just and harmonious social formations. The concept of social justice is one of the fruits of the search for an ideal social set up.

Barry (1981) holds that social justice requires that society, rather than just the actions of individuals be evaluated for its content of justice and injustice. Thus, the concept of social justice is an end-state, one that has been devised as a yardstick for measuring social life in terms of the extent to which principles of egalitarianism underscore social policy and administration. This means that theories of social justice place focus on the needs and wants of citizens and their satisfaction and assess the extent to which a society ranks in terms of attention paid to them. It means government must consciously establish a norm structure that reflects the provision of rights, privileges, and the satisfaction of interests. And judging by the fact that the natural requirements and needs of life are so many while resources are scare, it becomes easy to see why conflict-creating situations abound always. In the light of the need to ensure harmony and peace, the state is generally required to advance social welfare through deliberate interventionist action if need be. Eze (1984) describes how Tanzania entrenched the principles of social justice as the focus of its social and political philosophy as embodied in the Arusha Declaration which contains the following beliefs among others:

(1)   that all citizens together possess all natural resources of the country held in trust for their descendants;

(2)   that to ensure economic justice the state must have effective control of the principal means of production;

(3)   that it is the responsibility of the state to intervene actively in the economic life of the nation to prevent the accumulation of wealth to an extent which is inconsistent with the existence of a classless society p.112).

The foregoing principles of the Tanzanian Republic are ample testimony of the egalitarian focus of the principles of social justice. The concern with egalitarianism is meant to eliminate as much as possible, causes of strife, discontent, and conflict. It is also, on the other hand, meant to enhance happiness and fulfillment in the citizenry. To that extent, the end-state doctrine of social justice is akin to utilitarianism which seeks to enhance the overall good and happiness of the majority. Burns and Hart (1985) speak for Jeremy Bentham the apostle of utilitarianism when they quote him:

> An action that may be said to be conformable to the prin-
> ciple of utility (meaning with respect to the community at
> large) when the tendency it must augment the happiness
> of the community is greater than any it has to diminish it
> (p.272).

If utilitarianism is meant to eliminate pain, then we can conclude that justice and utility are fellow travelers having the same
end-state goal of social peace, harmony, and happiness. Thus,
in line with the foregoing ideas Aguda (1986) advocating social
justice in Nigeria declares.

> We cannot say that we are administering law and justice
> and shut our eyes to social and economic injustice around
> us. We must struggle to ensure that none of our citizens
> suffer unnecessarily form want of food, adequate hous-
> ing and clothing... There must be provision in the societal
> and economic structures for the lowest possible standard
> of living of the poorest members of the society. In other
> words, the difference between the wealthiest and the
> poorest citizen must be minimal (p.17).

He goes on to declare that until there is a good measure of
concern for the material welfare of every member of society,
the administration of justice cannot be in order. He clinches his
argument with the fact the economic condition of litigants in
civil and criminal litigation affects the "quality" of justice they
get. He then advocates a situation where the legal system can
be made to channel economic behaviour to some extent, so that
poverty can be checked and social institutions will gradually enhance positive patterns of social behaviour. In fact, for him: "The
proper reason for the very existences of law is justice not law-
yers' justice, but social and economic... justice... law to justify its
existence by justice, social justice, economic justice."

Aguda is not alone in applying the value of justice to the
social system of a community. Philip Petite (1981) describes the
role of the political philosopher as the assessment of available
options by specifying the demands or criteria of adjudication
so that the social philosopher becomes capable of determining

which one of the several competing options of social charter he should prefer. Justice therefore becomes the touchstone for identifying the ideal social formation. And since justice is based on the rational and universalizable principles of impartiality, non-arbitrariness, fairness, and reason, it becomes easy to see why every man can subscribe to it. Justice therefore, helps to locate the interests that a political charter should serve and the way such interests should be served. This is because by reason of the inherent logic of fairness to all parties the concept of justice is said to pick out "as optimal a charter which serves people's interest in some allegedly non-arbitrary way" (Petite, 1981, p.1).

John Rawls (1971) is about the most eloquent voice among present day advocates of social justice, that is, the idea of assessing social and economic arrangements and policies using the criterion of justice. Rawl (1971) goes on to identify the interests, which the charter of justice should serve among men. He even delineates the way it should serve them. He states:

A doctrine of political economy must include an interpretation of the public good which is based on a conception of justice. It is to guide the reflection of the citizen when he considers questions of economic and social policy. He is to take up the perspective of the constitutional convention or the legislative stage and ascertain how the principles of justice apply. A political opinion concerns what advocates the good of the body politic and invokes some criterion for the just division of social advantages (p. 259).

Rawls' ideas on justice run into a very elaborate manifesto of the ideal society. Based on the principle of catering for the interest of the worst underdog, he formulates a very novel idea which dwarfs utilitarianism as a moral theory. Rawls specifies equality in the assignment of basic rights and duties in any society while social and economic inequalities such as those of wealth and authority are regarded as just only if they result in compensating benefits for everyone especially the least advantaged members of society.

The primary role of justice as a social construct has also

been adumbrated by Harold Laski (1974). Quoting Henry Sidg-wick, he indicates:

> In determining a nation's rank in political civilization, no test is more decisive than the degree in which justice, as defined by the law, is realized in its judicial administration, both as between one private citizen and members of the government (p.54).

The above statement goes to underscore the cardinal import-ance of justice in every human society. Indeed, it is of utmost importance in the emergent states of renascent Africa because, with the culture clash between the western nation states and the ex-colonial territories, there is a great deal of confusion in the realm of values. This has created a void which needs to be filled by the proper articulation of social and moral values that con-duce to the growth of a viable political culture on the continent. In this direction, it is common knowledge that there has been a dearth of original and genuine political praxis on the content on which democracy can be firmly established. And, for as long as the understanding is still at a very low level, the doubtful moral texture of the political culture is not a good sign. Laski (1974:542) says: "When we know with some exactness how a nation-state dispenses justice we know with some exactness the moral character to which it can pretend"

A close look at a lot of African countries shows that the praxis of justice leaves much to be desired. Aguda (1986) has clearly examined the various ramifications of the problem in Ni-geria and summed up the situation as a "crisis". He declares with characteristic adroitness:

> ...no nation on earth can survive unless justice can reign supreme – not the sort of unequal justice we at present practice and feel proud of. What is required is equal justice based upon social justice... no democracy nor indeed mili-tary dictatorship can survive for long unless the people are assured not only of equal legal justice but also social just-ice. Government is not an end in itself; it is a means to an end. That justice is not legal justice but social justice (p. ix).

In the foregoing statement, Aguda (1986) rather overshoots the mark by declaring that the end of government is not legal justice, but social justice. The truth is that legal justice and social justice are but different aspects of the same concept. While it is true that legal justice can have real meaning mainly within the context of prevailing social justice, it is also true that the concept of social justice is a controversial and nebulous one. Indeed, there are very strong arguments against the concept that one would be hard put to ignore it totally.

One major exponent of the conservation school of thought on social justice is Hayek (1974). Declaring that social justice is a mirage, he advances very convincing arguments that it is just the thinking of a group of leftist ideologues which has little basis within a market economy where rigid prediction of end-purposes has no place. Hayek opines that it is not ideal to coerce people into rigid identical ends. It is only permissible for general welfare or public good. Hence government, in his opinion is required to secure conditions in which individuals and smaller groups of people will have favourable opportunities of mutually providing for their respective needs. He contends that civil authority should merely create conditions for the operation of the spontaneous order enabling individuals to provide for their needs in a manner not closely scrutinized by authority. This is the free market order or in which ends are many and separate. The essence of the market order is the striving for the results of social cooperation in the society. No single person is responsible for the results of a market order. Hayek feels that in such a situation, social justice as generally understood is only meaningful in a centrally planned, "command economy." Therefore, in a free society in which the positions of the various members do not depend on anybody's design, one cannot talk of principles of just conduct to bring about a "just" pattern of appropriation of benefits. He hinges his argument on the fact that:

> The demand for social justice is addressed not to the individual but to society - yet society, in the strict sense in which it must be distinguished from the apparatus of

government is incapable of acting for a specific purpose and the demand that the members of the society should organize themselves in a manner which makes it possible to assign particular shares of the product of society to the different individuals or groups. The primary question then becomes whether there exists a moral duty to submit to a power which can coordinate the efforts of the members of the society with the aim of achieving a pattern of distribution regarded as just (Hayek, 1974, p.64).

Hayek contends that the benefits of a market are not deliberately allocated as to exclude some while favouring others. Besides, they are not foreseen or intended but rather enhance the satisfaction of the varied needs of members of the society. According to him, it is therefore absurd to demand justice from such a process. In summary Hayek (1974) dismisses the entire social justice rhetoric as consisting of:

(a)   The dislike of people who are better off than oneself (envy)

(b)   Animosity towards great wealth

(c)   An attempt to despoil the rich because riches are outrageous.

He further concludes that although social justice is an innocent expression of goodwill towards the less fortunate, it is merely a device for protecting the entrenched interests of a group who want to impose their ideology over and above the general interests of others. For him social justice, conceived in the equalitarian sense, is a mask for socialism.

Many of the tenets of social justice theory seem to suggest some form of general control of the resources of the state in an end-state manner of social existence. Thus, as much as possible there should be equality in the appropriation of social goods and fundamental rights so that some do not unduly oppress weaker members of the society.

Conclusion

The foregoing excursion into the concept of social justice shows the extent to which philosophers have formulated principles aimed at prescribing how human society should be organized. The result has been a variety of approaches and solutions proffered for consideration and choice as to how social harmony would be promoted. In the Nigerian, nay the African context, it is obvious that national challenges of group oppression, religious extremism, lack of restructuring, political hypocrisy, social and political corruption, environmental injustice, regional divide (as in north/south divide in Nigeria) and its implications as well as intra-national challenges of militancy, secessionist agitations and similar social stresses do exist as a result of the lack of justice values in the body politic. It is hoped that these issues will be meaningfully confronted with philosophical thinking and the application of philosophy of education to a nation's public affairs.

References

Aguda, A. (1986). *The crisis of justice*. Akure: Eresu Hills Publishers.

Barry, N. (1981). *An introduction to modern political theory.* London: Macmillan

Bullivant, B. (1980). *The pluralist dilemma in education.* London: George Allen & Unwin Ltd.

Burns, B., & Hart, A. (1985). Extracts from Bentham's *An introduction to the principles of morals and legislation*. In A. Lloyd and B. Freeman. *Introduction to jurisprudence*. London: Stevens & Sons Ltd.

Eze, O. (1984) *Human rights in Africa.* Lagos/Ibadan: Macmillan-NIIA.

Federal Republic of Nigeria (2014). *National policy on education.* Lagos: NERDC Press.

Gana, J. (1989). *MAMSER directorate: Political education manual.* Abuja: DSM.

Hayek, F. A. (1976). *The mirage of social justice.* London: Routledge & Kegan Paul.

Laski, H. (1934/74): *A grammar of politics.* Oxford: Clarendon Press.

Lucas, J. R. (1980). *On justice.* Oxford: Clarendon Press

Rawls, J. (1971). *A theory of justice:* Cambridge, Massachusetts: Belknap Press

Petite, P. (1981). *Judging justice.* London: Routledge & Kegan Paul.

CHAPTER 12

PROFESSIONAL STANDARDS AND THE REGULATION OF THE TEACHING PROFESSION IN NIGERIA

Professor Addison Mark WOKOCHA
Former Registrar/Chief Executive
Teachers Registration Council of Nigeria
Abuja

Abstract

The paper presents a comprehensive view of the concept, purpose, evolution, and structure of the Professional Standards for Nigerian Teachers. It gives an overview of TRCN contributions at both international and national levels towards introducing and institutionalizing the Professional Standards. Finally, it discusses impediments to the implementation of the Standards in Nigeria and how these could be overcome.

Introduction

P rofessional standards or benchmarks are imperative for every profession to deliver services that meet both the tangible and ethical needs of society. Teaching is said to be the mother of all the other noble professions because it educates and raises members of these other professions. In other words, no one could be a professional without first passing through the tutelage of a teacher. Therefore, teaching is not only the pivot of development but also the very "birth place of other professions". In this respect, professional standards for the teaching profession is not only indispensable but also an aggregation and robust encapsulation of the finest standards of other professions and indeed, society itself.

It is also commonly said that the school is a microcosm of society because the school is just a chip of society and mirrors the cultural and developmental aspirations of the people. For this reason, the development and enforcement of standards for the teaching profession are serious and fundamental issues because the standards are required to perfectly guide all professional duties and actions towards these societal, cultural and developmental aspirations. Thus, no profession can rise above the quality of its standards and a profession without standards is like a ship off there in the ocean without a compass or point of reference.

In recognition of the full implications and imperativeness of standards for any noble profession, the Teachers Registration Council of Nigeria (TRCN) as the apex professional regulatory agency for the teaching profession has in the last seven years facilitated the evolution of one of Nigeria's finest codes of professional standards, and indeed one of the best codes of standards anywhere in the world because the standards incorporated the best and latest standards operating in the teaching profession around the world today. The *Professional Standards for Nigerian*

Teachers presented to the public on March 11 by the Honourable Minister of Education, Professor Ruqayyatu Ahmed Rufa'i (OON) in Abuja was a watershed in the regulation and control of the teaching profession in Nigeria. The document, listed by the Honourable Minister as one of the legacies of her first term in office, has put the teaching profession in Nigeria on the same pedestal with the best of the world's professions. The Code with eighty-four (84) standards has laid the foundation for the separation of professionals from quacks, and from what is in consonance with the ethics of the profession and what is not. This paper therefore attempts to give a conceptual framework for the professional standards in the teaching profession overview of the evolution of the standards, anatomy of the standards, what TRCN as a professional regulatory agency intends to achieve with the standards, the challenges and way forward.

A Conceptual Note On Professional Standards In The Teaching Profession

Professional standards are important framework or benchmark within which professionals carry out their professional obligations and duties. They are usually coded and standardized instruments or documents that clearly and precisely define what the professional must know and put into practice and the core values, ideals and conduct that the professional must exhibit. ***Professional Standards*** therefore refer *to a minimum set of knowledge, skills, values, attitude, conduct, rights, privileges and obligations expected of a professional.* (TRCN 2010).

The *Professional Standards for Nigerian Teachers* are derived from numerous national and international *benchmark documents,* legal frameworks and *education policies* intended to guide the general citizenry and the Education and practice of teachers in Nigeria and in the international community. Therefore, among the foundation documents of the *Professional Standards for Nigerian Teachers* are the Teachers Registration Council of Nigeria (TRCN) Act Cap T3 of 2004; Education (National Minimum Standards and Establishment of Institutions) Act Cap E3 of 1993; The Constitution of the Federal Republic of Nigeria 1999; The National Economic Empowerment and Development Strategy; The National Policy on Education (2008); The National Teacher Education Policy (2009); UNESCO/ILO Position on the Status of the Teacher; United Nations Declaration on Human Right, 1948; The Corrupt Practices and Other Related Offences Act, 2000 of Nigeria; The Child Rights Act, 2003 of Nigeria; Financial Regulations of the Federal Republic of Nigeria, 2000; The Public Service Rules of the Federal Republic of Nigeria, 2000; The Roadmap to the Education Sector in Nigeria, 2009 and so forth.

Purpose/Benefits Of The Professional Standards For Nigerian Teachers

The *Professional Standards for Nigerian teachers* exist primarily to help the relevant authorities to determine the professional standing of teachers. The professional standing in this context refers to the quality of the teacher as a professional, how fit the teacher is to teach, and the overall value of the teacher to the profession, the education system and entire society.

Therefore, the Professional Standards constitute a valid mechanism for separating professionals from quacks, for sorting and sieving the 'chaffs from the grains', for rewarding and placing sanctions on teachers, and for making other critical decisions relating professional and career prospects of teachers. For instance, using the Standards as benchmarks, authorities could determine training needs, promotability, ability to occupy certain leadership positions, suitability to teach at a level of the education system, and general prospects of career advancement among teachers. Indeed, it is expected that in due course, the employers of teachers would no longer promote teachers based purely on their annual performance evaluation scores but also on their Professional Standards scores obtained using the performance evaluation instrument attached to the Professional Standards. The Standards equally serve as self-assessment instrument which teachers could use to gauge and monitor their performance in the profession to take proactive actions to remedy their deficiencies and accelerate their career and professional advancement.

Importantly, the Professional Standards for Nigerian Teachers clearly specifies, codifies and criminalizes acts that amount to professional misconduct, negligence and incompetence. It integrates all aspects of the Teachers Codes of Conduct and establishes procedures for addressing any breach of the Codes. The Standards underscores the importance of the Teachers Investigating Panels established in all states of the Federation and Federal Capital Territory and the Teachers Tribunal domiciled at the TRCN Headquarters. The Standards vest in the Panels and Tribunal the power to investigate and punish breaches of all cases of professional misconduct, negligence and incompetence as provided in the TRCN Act Cap T3 of 2004.

At the international level, the Professional Standards for Nigerian Teachers helps Nigeria particularly the TRCN to report objectively on the professional standing of teachers as required by the Africa Forum of Teaching Regulatory Authorities (AFTRA) and International (World) Forum of Teaching Regulatory Authorities (IFTRA). Nigeria is a member of both AFTRA and IFTRA through the active participation of TRCN and in fact, TRCN is the Headquarters of AFTRA. These world bodies have brought many countries of the world together to work jointly to improve the dignity and conditions of migrant teachers and only teachers whose countries (through the teaching councils) give favourable letter of credence (letter of professional standing) could benefit from this international dignity and better working conditions abroad. The letter or report of professional standing must also be based on qualitative internationally accepted Professional Standards or benchmarks such as the Professional Standards for Nigerian Teachers. In writing letters of professional standing, AFTRA and IFTRA also expect the teaching councils to carry out background checks and criminal clearance of the teachers who wish to teach abroad. In essence, the existence and enforcement of an internationally acceptable professional standards are among the evidences required by the international community in assessing the quality, dignity and treatment that teachers who intend to teach or work abroad deserve.

The Evolution Of Professional Standards For Teachers In Nigeria

TRCN as the apex regulatory authority of the teaching profession in Nigeria has been mindful of its mandates and pursuing them with vigour since it commenced operations in 2000. Over the years as it recorded landmark achievements in the registration of teachers, continuous professional development, enforcement of professional ethics, and others, it recognized the need to come up with a very comprehensive internationally acclaimed framework to determine overall professional aspirations, quality and characteristics of the Nigerian teachers. Beginning from 2005 therefore, it initiated concrete steps to develop the Professional Standards for Nigerian teachers, which eventually passed through three key phases before its launch in 2011 by the Honourable Minister of Education, Professor Ruqayyatu Ahmed Rufa'i (OON).

The year 2005 witnessed the first phase as TRCN worked with other teaching councils around the world to institutionalize the concept of Professional Standards for the teaching profession. From that time, TRCN began working conscientiously towards introducing the concept of professional standards to the teaching profession in Nigeria. This first phase was marked by TRCN's collation of the relevant literature and best practices around the world on Professional Standards and initial efforts to develop the Standards.

In 2006, TRCN moved into the second phase as it joined efforts with then the Honourable Minister of Education, Mrs. Obiageli Ezekwesili to make Professional Standards for Nigeria Teachers one of the key aspects of the Education Reform in Nigeria of the then Federal Government. The Minister therefore created a Ministerial *Teacher Quality Task Team* whose duty was to work with TRCN to fully develop a Professional Standards for Nigerian Teachers. The Task Team was chaired by the Director/Chief Executive of the National Teachers Institute, Kaduna, with the TRCN Registrar/Chief Executive as Secretary. The Team within its limited time of operation produced a valuable draft Professional Standards for teachers.

The valedictory stage in the development of the Standards came in 2010-2011 when TRCN engaged the services of a consultant, a renowned Professor of Education, Professor J. D. Okoh to mid-wife the development of the standards as it is today. The document therefore passed through enrichment by a consultant, then was subjected to critique of a core group of experts, later validated by a national stakeholders' forum and passed through the rest of the statutory requirements which included approval by TRCN Governing Board.

Anatomy Of The Professional Standards For Ni-

gerian Teachers

The Professional Standards for Nigerian Teachers covers four thematic areas, namely:

1. Professional Knowledge - The things the teacher must know,
2. Professional Skills - The practical ability that the teachers must exhibit,
3. Professional Values, Attitude and Conduct - The mode of behaviour, thought, words and action that may or may not be associated with teachers, and
4. Professional Membership Obligations - Responsibilities of teachers towards the profession, the professional regulatory agency and related matters.

Additionally, the document also avails teachers of vital information such as:

1. Guidelines on Induction at Point of Graduation – The concept, modalities and benefits of admitting fresh Education graduates into the teaching profession before discharging them from the training institutions.
2. Guidelines on Continuous Professional Development (CPD) – Nature and implications of professional development activities and life-long capacity building expected of teachers.
3. Instruments for Assessment of Teachers' Professional Standing – A valid and reliable instrument for assessment of a teacher professional standing in a matter that national and international comparisons are possible and useful.

The four thematic areas listed above altogether have 36 Sub-Themes, giving rise to 84 Standards. TRCN has classified teachers in Nigeria into four categories as shown below, therefore different level of performance is expected from each category with respect to the 84 Standards.

Table 1

Categorization of Teachers in Nigeria

Category	Qualifications
A	PhD in Education or PhD in other fields plus teaching qualification such as Nigeria Certificate in Education, Professional Diploma in Education or Post Graduate Diploma in Education.
B	Master's degree in education or Master's degree in other fields plus teaching qualification such as Nigeria Certificate in Education, Professional Diploma in Education or Post Graduate Diploma in Education.
C	Bachelor's Degree in education or Bachelor's Degree in other fields plus teaching qualification such as Nigeria Certificate in Education, Professional Diploma in Education or Post Graduate Diploma in Education.
D	Nigeria Certificate in Education

The relationship between the themes, sub-themes and Standards are sketched below:

Fig 1: A diagrammatic sketch of the Professional Standards for Nigerian Teachers

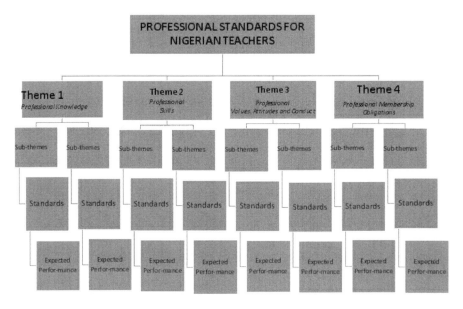

Source: TRCN Professional Standards (2012, p. 16)

Table 2
How Performance for Each of the 84 Standards
Vary Across the Categories of Teachers

STAND-ARDS	EXPECTED PERFORMANCE			
	NCE Teachers (CATEGORY D)	Graduate Teachers (CATEGORY C)	Master Teachers (CATEGORY B)	Doctoral Teachers (CATEGORY A)
KNOWLEDGE: Sub-Theme 1: Subject content				
Standard 1: Teachers know the content of the subjects they teach.	Teachers' knowledge covers all the themes and topics stipulated in the subject curriculum issued by the appropriate	The same. For instance, a teacher of Mathematics at Senior Secondary Education level is expected to know all the	Teachers know their specialized teaching subjects and know all the relevant themes and topics prescribed by the Min-	Teachers know all the themes and topics in their specialized teaching subjects prescribed by the Minimum Academic Standards

	curriculum authority. For instance, a teacher in a Basic School is expected to know all the subjects, themes and topics in the Basic School Curriculum issued by the NERDC.	themes and topics stipulated in the curriculum of Senior Secondary School Mathematics issued by NERDC, JAMB, NECO, WAEC, and other relevant authorities at that level.	imum Academic Standards for the subjects.	and have advanced knowledge of these subjects based on recent theories and research findings.

Source: Professional Standards (TRCN 2012, pp. 26-28)

Challenges In Implementing The Standards And Way Forward

Though a great innovation in the regulation of the teaching profession in Nigeria, the implementation of the Standards is not without challenges. A few of the challenges may therefore be mentioned here.

Basically, the Standards require continuous evaluation and support of the teachers across the length and breadth of the country by TRCN. With the large size of Nigeria as a geographical entity that has numerous transport and communication difficulties, and with teachers being the largest professional group in Nigeria, reaching every teacher in Nigeria effectively is a logistical nightmare. Every Nigerian teacher deserves to have a copy of the Standards free of charge as ignorance is not excuse under the law. Every teacher and indeed the generality of stakeholders also deserve to be adequately sensitized as the concept of Professional Standards is still new and even strange to most teachers and stakeholders. However, the cost of producing and distributing copies of the Standards and organizing sensitization/capacity building programmes for teachers and other stakeholders in Nigeria is well beyond the poor budgetary funding received by TRCN and especially when other competing needs are taken into consideration. Therefore, the implementation of the Standards is greatly being hampered by funding in the light of the factors enumerated above. While increased budgetary allocation from National Appropriation will go a long way in alleviating the situation, teachers themselves will also be greatly assisting to overcome the situation by dutifully paying their annual dues as funds from teachers' registration and dues are usually ploughed back by TRCN into meeting teachers' needs.

The varying levels of cooperation among states and employers of teachers with regards to national policies poses its own challenge. While virtually all the states of the Federation politically and publicly declare their support for quality teachers and the professionalization of teaching, only very few states significantly implement the policies. Most states simply lack the political will to enforce policies meant to promote the teaching profession. Some even see teaching as dumping ground for compensating political stooges to the point that the National Policy on Education which states that the Nigeria Certificate in Education shall be the minimum teaching qualification (a policy that came into effect since 1977) has not been reasonably accomplished in most states of the Federation. Giving the lack of political will and the politicization of education, it may be an up-hill task for most states to adopt and implement the Standards faithfully as the primary document for the regulation of teachers in their domain. Here again, TRCN will continue to push forward dialogue aimed at sensitizing the public particularly governments and employers of teachers. Currently, some states have even on their own decided to introduce professional competency examinations for their teachers without reference either to the Professional Standards for Nigerian Teachers or the statutory mandates of TRCN responsible by law to set standards for the teaching profession and to raise those standards from time to time. Governments therefore will need to accord TRCN its statutory recognition and to work with it in all matters that come under its statutory purview. Some of the teachers themselves as well have poor understanding of the powers and relevance of TRCN as the teachers or their unions in the states enmeshed in the professional competency test have not bothered to either report to TRCN or seek any form of resolution of the matter under the TRCN umbrella.

Employers of teachers have not paid adequate attention to improving the working conditions of teachers. The debilitating and dehumanizing conditions under which teachers work have over the years obliterated the self-worth, professional dignity and motivation of teachers. Teachers' compliance with the provisions of the Professional Standards depends largely on the teachers' socio-economic well-being, quality of working environment, support services available and the enthusiasm of the teachers as professionals. When teachers are not enthusiastic about their profession because there is virtually nothing to celebrate about the profession, their spirit and morale are dampened, and they are not motivated to aspire to the stipulated professional ideals. When teachers stay many years without initial teacher education without any continuous professional development programme, their knowledge of subject matter, skills, and even attitudes plummet leading to retarded behavioural or performance outcomes, and in some cases attrition or labour turnover. If such conditions persist, entrenching the Professional Standards in the education system will be difficult. Therefore, all stakeholders including teachers' unions, non-governmental organizations, international development partners, must initiate and sustain advocacy and pressure for the improvement of teachers' working condition in Nigeria. Teachers must also work on their psyche to improve their self-perception because it is difficult to emancipate an individual who has the wrong view and attitude towards oneself.

Conclusion

The introduction of the Professional Standards in the teaching profession in Nigeria is a watershed in the drive to raise the quality, dignity, and rewards of Nigerian teachers to international standards. TRCN has as the professional regulatory agency for the teaching profession in Nigeria has been the vanguard for the Standards. With the launching of the Standards by the Minister of Education as part of the key achievement of her administration in 2010-2011, teachers have been empowered and given a mechanism to distinguish between professionals and quacks and to distinguish between those that deserve rewards as professionals and those that deserve sanctions. It is time therefore for all teachers, governments, employers of teachers and other stakeholders to rise up and collaborate with TRCN towards making the maximum use of the instrument - the *Professional Standards for Nigerian Teachers.*

References

Federal Republic of Nigeria (1993). *Teachers Registration Council of Nigeria Act No. 31*, Supplement to Official Gazette Extraordinary pp. A285-A302. Lagos: Federal Government Press.

Federal Republic of Nigeria (1993). *Education (national minimum standards and establishment of institutions) act.* Lagos: Federal Government Press.

Federal Republic of Nigeria (1999). *Constitution of the Federal Republic of Nigeria 1999.* Lagos: Federal Government Press.

Federal Republic of Nigeria (2000). *The corrupt practices and other related offences act 2000.* Ibadan: University Press Plc.

Federal Republic of Nigeria (2000). *Financial regulations (Revised to 1st January 2000).* Lagos: Federal Government Press.

Federal Republic of Nigeria (2000). *Public service rules (Revised to 1st January 2000).* Lagos: Federal Government Press.

Federal Republic of Nigeria (2007). *National economic empowerment and development strategy (NEEDS).* Abuja: National Planning Commission.

Federal Republic of Nigeria (2008). *National policy on education.* Abuja: NERDC Press.

Federal Ministry of Education (2009). *National teacher education pol-*

icy. Abuja: FME

Federal Ministry of Education (2009). *Roadmap to the education sector in Nigeria.* Abuja: FME

National Commission for Colleges of Education (2009). *Minimum standards for NCE teachers: General education.* (4th ed.). Abuja: NCCE

National Universities Commission (2007). *Benchmark minimum academic standards for undergraduate programmes in Nigerian universities: Education.* Abuja: FME

New Institute of Teachers (2009). *Professional teaching standards.* New South Wales, Australia.

New Institute of Teachers (2009). *Continuing professional development: Maintaining accreditation at professional competence.* New South Wales, Australia.

New Institute of Teachers (2009). *Accreditation at professional leadership: Information for candidates.* New South Wales, Australia.

New Institute of Teachers (2009). *Accreditation at professional accomplishment: Information for candidates.* New South Wales, Australia.

New Jersey Department of Education (2004). *New Jersey professional standards for teachers and school leaders.* Trenton, New Jersey: Author. (http//:www.state.nj.us/education)

Nigerian Educational Research and Development Council (2007). *9-year basic education curriculum.* Lagos: NERDC Printing Press.

Nigerian Educational Research and Development Council (2007). *Senior secondary education curriculum.* Lagos: NERDC Printing Press.

Institute of Chartered Accountants of Nigeria (2001). *Handbook.* Lagos: Derate Nigeria Ltd.

New Zealand Teachers Council (1997). *Handbook: The registration of teachers.* Aotearoa.

New Zealand Teachers Council (2002). *Guidelines for the approval of teacher education programmes.* Aotearoa.

Ontario College of Teachers (2002). *Accreditation of teacher education programmes.* Made under the *Ontario College of Teachers Act, 1996.* The Ontario Gazette, Ontario Regulation 347/02.

Ontario College of Teachers (2002). Teacher qualifications. Made under the *College of teachers act, 1996 –   Ontario Regulation 184/97 Amended to Ontario regulation 50/04: Teacher qualifications.*

Ontario College of Teachers (2004). *Foundations of professional practice.* Toronto: Author.

Ontario College of Teachers (2006). *Leadership excellence responsibility.*

Toronto.

Ontario College of Teachers (2006). *Professional advisory: Additional qualifications – Extending professional knowledge.* Toronto.

Ontario Province of Canada (1996). *Ontario college of teachers act, 1996.*Toronto.

Ontario Ministry of Education (2002). *Supporting teacher excellence: Teacher performance appraisal manual and approved forms and guidelines.* Toronto. (www.edu.gov.on.ca)

Palmer, Carolyn (2010). *Teacher professional standards: The views of highly accomplished special education teachers.* Flinders, Australia: Flinders University. (Carolyn.palmer@flinders.edu.au).

Pharmacists Council of Nigeria (2000). *Mandatory continuing educational programme for recertification of pharmacists.* Lagos: Dott K. Ventures (Nig) Ltd.

Pharmacists Council of Nigeria (2005). *Mandatory continuing professional development programme for re-certification of pharmacists.* Lagos.

Queensland College of Teachers (2006). *Professional standards for Queensland teachers.* Toowong, Australia. (www.qct.edu.au)

Republic of South Africa (2000). *South African council for educators act No. 31 of 2000.* Government Gazette Registered at the Post Office as a Newspaper, Cape Town, 2 August 2000, Vol. 422 No. 21431.

South African Council for Educators (2005). *Code of professional ethics.* Pretoria.

Supreme Court of Arizona, United States of America (2001). Rule 45 on *Mandatory continuing legal education.*

Teachers Registration Board of South Australia (1999). *Annual report.* South Australia.

Teachers Registration Council of Nigeria (2007). *Professional diploma in education: National minimum standards.* Abuja: Mbawa Communications Resources Ltd.

Teachers Registration Council of Nigeria (2010). *Professional standards for Nigerian teachers.* Abuja: TRCN

The Professional Academy for Teachers in Egypt (2008). *Introduction.* Cairo. (http://pat.moe.gov.eg)

The Teaching Council of Ireland (2009). *Codes of professional conduct for teachers.* Kildare: Maynooth, Co. Kildare.

Teacher Training Agency, London (2002). *Qualifying to teach: Professional standards for qualified teacher status and recruitments for initial teacher training.* London.

Training and Development Agency for Schools, London (2006). *Profes-*

sional standards for teachers: Why sit still in your career? London. (or www.tda.gov.uk/standards)

UNESCO (2002). *Information and communication technology in education: A Curriculum for schools and programmes of teacher development.* Paris: UNESCO Division of Higher Education.

United Kingdom (1998). *Teaching and higher education act* c. 30.

United Nations (1948). *Universal declaration of human rights.* Adopted and Proclaimed by the General Assembly Resolution 217A of December 10, 1948.

Author acknowledges the contributions of the Teachers Registration Council of Nigeria, the Otonti Nduka Foundation for Values Education and the Nigerian Academy of Education.

addisonmark@yahoo.com

CHAPTER 13

ADOLESCENTS AND VALUE ISSUES

Queen. I. OBINAJU
Professor of Early Childhood Education
University of Uyo
Uyo

Introduction

V alues and ethics are principles held high in any society. These include the ingredients of socialization and education of essentially the young in any given society. At some point, adults too need to be reminded of the values of the society especially when it is noticed that the adult in question is falling short of expectation. When values are properly cultivated into citizens, the result is a stable society. In other words, it can be said that instability in any society can be traced to faulty and incomplete socialization and education especially as regards the values of the society in question.

The above discussion suggests that values are society specific. This means that values depend on the society in question. However, there are some common threads which run through most of the known human communities of the world. Taking

Nigeria as our example, values held high include among others respect for elders, obedience to authority, honesty, justice, hard work, patience, tolerance and kindness. These are taught to citizens through traditional institutions, formal and informed education. Fafunwa (1974), Ojoade (2004), and Uyoata (2006) discuss the use of proverbs in ensuring proper inculcation of values in citizens.

Teaching of values is continuous. It starts from birth and is intensified during childhood and adolescent stages of development. After these stages, non- adherence to values is frowned at and invokes some surprise in observers. This paper intends to examine the adolescent stage of development and the extent to which adolescents have acquired values of the society. Are there certain encumbrances in the society? Are there certain encumbrances which may impede acquisition of values at this stage? How can they be overcome?

Who Is An Adolescent?

An adolescent is a human being whose chronological age falls between 11 and 18 years. This is the period between childhood and adulthood. In the eyes of the child, the adolescent is matured. There is no difference between him and the adult. Therefore, the child looks up to the adolescent for guidance. For the adult, the adolescent is immature; he is an over grown child who still needs a lot of guidance. This singular phenomenon places the adolescent in a dilemma of being termed an adult at some of the times and a child at other times. To the adolescent himself, he sees himself as no longer a child and desires to be treated as such. However, at the face of some societal exigencies, he discovers that he may not be as experienced as an adult. Here he finds himself at cross roads.

Physically, the adolescent grows rapidly, replacing childhood features with adult ones. For girls, the adolescent resembles an adult as she reaches adult height and weight during this period. The boy may still grow and reach adult height in his twenties. There are also changes in several energy potentials.

The adolescent grows steadily stronger and experiences sexual maturity. While the girl experiences evolution and menstrual flow, the boy experience production of sperms and occasional wet dreams. These occurrences trigger of sexual excitement and / or embarrassment depending on how the adolescent handless the urge.

Socially the adolescent is seen enjoying the company of his peers and seeking less dependence on parent. At this point peer standards have serious regulatory effect on his life and behaviour. Adults tend to term this tendency a revolt or a non-conforming attitude. Emotionally, adolescents are seen not going in the way they expect. They are impatient, excited as well as easily irritated. All these attributes of the adolescent often throw the adolescent into problems with the society.

Challenges Of The Adolescent

Chauhan (1996), Obinaju (2011) and Biehler and Snowman (1982) all enumerate several challenges faced by the adolescent arising from his physique, peer pressure and the like. These include the problem which arises from the assertive nature of the adolescent. Noticing that he is now an adult, he forces himself to be heard. This new form of self-expression is often interpreted to be aggression. Because of the new development in the physical appearance of the adolescent, the maturity of several developmental organs of the adolescent, he faces new challenges in the area of sanitation. He needs to clean up his armpits, pubic hairs, shave facial hair and cope with excessive sweating. For girls, there arises the need to be neat about her menstrual period and other bodily development. These make the adolescent tend to be self-conscious.

Furthermore, the adolescent is worried about her appearance and health. This makes him to take extra care of his dressing, watch what he eats and his outward representation. He accepts compliments with delight. He appreciates such compliments as "you are beautiful / handsome" or "strong/courageous" etc. The desire to be complimented makes him fall prey easily to sweet tongued flatters. In the case of girls, this tendency may result in teenage pregnancy, falling in love and some uncontrolled excesses. For boys, it manifests in a form of truancy.

The home no longer provides any charm for the adolescent. He prefers the company of peers who are themselves immature. Experiences shared in these circles are held high in the mind of the adolescent. Sometimes the stories he listens to mislead him and he may not have enough courage to confirm them. This situation is compounded when the home is unfavorable. Home situations referred to here may include broken home; a home where harsh and disgraceful punishments are common features and the like.

The adolescent is known to be assertive, pushful and impatient especially when he has a point to make and especially when the case concerns his well-being. This attributed is often frowned at by adult. They are known to exaggerate emotions. They can laugh very loudly at a slight tickle and swift to a depressed mood within a short space of time. They do not mind weeping loudly when provoked. These may be socially interpreted either as a misbehaviour or as a disturbance depending of course on the circumstance.

Adolescents toward 18-29 years are known to worry about marriage, examination and success. They act out several stories they have been hearing and, in most circumstances, this lands them in trouble. Embarrassed by the outcome of their numerous experiments, they tend to abuse drugs. Drugs known to be abused by adolescents include antibiotics, alcohol and marijuana. Drug abuse normally comes as an escape from frustration, self-misuse and the impending consequences.

Other sources of worry for the adolescent include choice of vocation, confusion about societal code of conduct and maintenance of relationship. Quite often what he acquired through formal medium of instruction like school, church and parental advice are at variance with the practices observed within the wider society. He observes people cheating out on others at the slightest opportunity. He becomes afraid and confused. He finds it difficult to reconcile both tendencies and take a decision on which mode to adopt.

Marrying early or late also poses its own challenge on the adolescent. Early maturing girls tend to be shy as the features of maturity become obvious quite early in life while late maturing girls still have a little more time to play baby. In the case of boys, early maturing boys are easily singled out and given leadership roles. They therefore become more responsible and are often bossy. Late maturing boys also play boy until later in life. These challenges taken comprehensively have implications for value inculcation and value maintenance in the society especially in this new millennium.

Adolescent Challenges And The Issue Of Values In The Society

As observed in our earlier discussion, values are uncompromised standards in the society. The society takes defined steps to inculcate these in the young to ensure that they are maintained and kept. Uyoata (2006) and Ojoade (2004) advocate that we should use proverbs to teach our children values. With the challenges of the adolescent discussed above, the actions of the adolescent in several circumstances can be interpreted as low in values. An instance would be when the adolescent asserts himself; talks defiantly before an adult to drive home his point. In the face of a disagreement, he could shout out, cry or exhibit his physical strength. At such an occurrence he would be insulting, lacking respect for an elder and delinquent. Once labeled, the adolescent makes no further attempt to live on the positive line. A situation, if not checked could make him, perpetrate evil.

Possibly intolerant, or should he, out of anxiety over examination and success, indulge in examination malpractice, the value of the society- honesty and hard work to achieve success would suffer. In these and many other ways, the adolescent stage has been associated with low values and the following are often cited; low morality, truancy, dishonesty, impatience, lack of respect and the like. These assertions are often made basing the judgment on the interpretation of the adult.

If properly interpreted in many cases, the adolescent may not be low in values. On the other hand, there are adolescents who are very strict on values maintenance and societal orders. These are those whose socialization process was also very strict and uncompromising. Weighing these occurrences and in the face of the new millennium when social vices also are on the increase, what should be the approach so that we ensure that Nigerian adolescents live to uphold and sustain Nigerian values?

Towards Positive Values In Adolescents

To every learning activity there is a critical period. Appreciating positive values is started very early in life. When this is the case, there would not arise a situation whereby, the adolescent becomes confused on what is accepted and what is not in the society. When inculcation is systematic and consistently carried out, it would lack pressure. Therefore, the tendency for the child/adolescent to kick against it would be almost nonexistent.

We should not be deceived that every home can inculcate the right type of values. Many homes are quite deficient. This places the onus on the state to ensure the inculcation of the right type of values in the youth. Towards assuring this, institutionalization of youths is recommended. This leads this discussion to recommend reintroduction of boarding schools to ensure the inculcation of the right type of values in the youths. Even when the home had started on a wrong footing, it can be corrected with institutionalization and proper supervision.

As recommended by the behaviorists; (Skinner, Pavlov and Bandura), incentives and rewards rather than threat and punishment should be the preferred method so that the adolescent sees constant exhibition of the right type of value as contingent upon receiving a reward and not an avoidance of punishment.

Finally, adults should be counselled to be tolerant of adolescent occasional slips. They should be reminded that adolescents are very sensitive to criticisms and reproach. Corrections in love and encouragement would ensure restoration rather than outright rebuke and scorn.

Conclusion

This discussion has highlighted what is meant by values, the adolescent, his life and characteristics. The adolescent had been seen as being peculiar as he has several challenges arising from his peculiarity. Often these challenges push him to exhibit behaviours which could lead one to assess him as low in values. These when properly handled could restore the adolescent citizen. Ways of ensuring that the adolescent imbibes and maintains high values of the society have been suggested. If these steps are taken, the incidences of adolescents displaying behaviors which suggest that they are low in values would be greatly reduced

References

Biehler, R. F., & Snowman, J. (1982). *Psychology applied to teaching.* Boston: Houghton Mifflin.

Chauhan, S. S. (1996). *Advanced educational psychology.* Delhi: Vikas Publishing House.

Fafunwa, A. B. (1974). *History of Nigerian education.* London: George Allen & Unwin Ltd.

Obinaju, Q. I. (2011). Peer group influence. In A. E. Udosen., D. E. Oko. & I. E. Ekanem (Eds.). *Life and academic reflections of Professor Queen Idongesit Obinaju.* Lagos: Ivy Press Ltd.

Obinaju, Q. I. (2011). Equipping the 21st century girl-child, ibid.

Ojoade, J. O (2004) Internationalism rooted in proverbs: Proverbs rooted of internationalism. 13th Inaugural lecture. University of Jos.

Uyoata, U. E. (2006). Inculcating values in the Nigerian child. Let us adopt proverbs and metaphors as strategies.

CHAPTER 14

THE PLACE OF MORAL EDUCATION IN THE NIGERIAN EDU-CATION SYSTEM

Dr. (Mrs.) I. A. BEBEBIAFIAI
Federal College of Education (Technical)
Omoku, Rivers State

Introduction

A very important aspect of the development of human personality is moral development. Omoregbe (1990) opines that moral development and maturity of citizens are pre-requisites for the development of that society. He also holds the opinion that to remove morality from society is to destroy it, for it will immediately cease to exist. To him, "the prosperity of a society depends on the moral disposition of its members." It is necessary to recall that Socrates, Plato, and Aristotle had emphasized the concept of morality.

Traditional education aims at inculcating a high degree of morality among the young children in our various communities. Christian and Islamic education emphasize the development of moral training in their adherents, as fundamental educational training to be received by them so as to be useful to themselves and society. And the National Policy on Education (2004) stresses the importance of developing good ethics in students and pupils when it states in Section 3 (3) that the inculcation of "moral and spiritual values in interpersonal and human relation" is part of national education philosophy and policy.

Maduka (1994) is also of the view that a critical look at the history of education would show that the twin competing educational aims had always been the cultivation of the intellect and training of character. Regrettably, in Nigeria today emphasis is placed more on academic qualifications leaving out the moral aspect. Over the years, the incidence of immorality among Nigerians appears to be on the upswing. Thus, bribery and corruption seem to be the norm; stealing, armed robbery, kidnapping, assassination, examination malpractice, cultism, prostitution, morbid struggle for material things, drug abuse, and disrespect for constituted authorities among other social ills.

It is the position of this paper that a key approach to tackling and solving the decadence in the Nigerian society is moral education. This has been the case from antiquity as enunciated by ancient philosophers. They held that every advancement in knowledge has practical bearing on life, either on the material or on the mental aspect. Knowledge which education brings provides how society can be changed for the better. Thus, the educational system of any nation and its curriculum should be reviewed from time to time to suit changes in the society.

Aminigo (2006) holds that morality is the force or the thread that binds social actions, social existence, and social relations. In addition, morality is an integral aspect of our make-up as human-beings, and so without morality there could be chaos in human society. The idea of morality therefore is tied up with the need to avoid the evils of the state of nature. Viewed from the above backdrop, the need for sound moral education in the Nigerian education system can be established even as an imperative. Indeed, morality and moral education are the very essence of human relations.

This paper reviews the concept of morality in Nigerian schools in the past, morality in Nigerian schools today, and discusses the need for inclusion of moral education in the Nigerian school curriculum. It offers suggestions for the effectiveness of the proposed programme of moral education in the school system.

Moral Education

Moral education is the type of education which inculcates in the learners the right type of values and attitudes necessary for coping with the ever-increasing moral problems brought about by increase in political, economic, and technological changes in society. Page and Thomas (1979) in Opajoba (1997) define it as "teaching or instruction in morals or ethical codes of conduct." The morals and ethics are not limited to the ones derivable from religious codes.

Moral education can also be the process of helping man to form good habits, characteristics, and experiences capable of making him live a useful, functional, and harmonious life as a member of a social group or society. It is the kind of education or training that is given to people for them to live a moral life, that will benefit them and their society, so that they could live a happy and harmonious life (Uchenna, 2006).

There is more to moral education than moral training or instruction. The word education is an important concept when discussing moral education. Peters (1966) in Anyacho (2001) notes that what distinguishes education from other activities that involve teaching is its emphasis on the development of understanding or critical awareness and appreciation of values and the ability to think for one's self. Moral education develops learners in the understanding of the right type of values as well as a critical awareness of the implications of moral actions while equipping them with the ability to make good moral choices and reach their own moral conclusions in a society that regularly offers them a variety of situations. Moral development is the quality of people's thinking on moral issues. It recognizes the moral autonomy of the individual and equips them with the basic tools for making moral choices or taking morally appropriate actions.

Objectives Of Moral Education In Nigeria

The basic aim of moral education is to create in the child's consciousness:

1. An interest in and favourable attitude towards morality.
2. An understanding of the nature and purpose of public morality.
3. An understanding of the criteria of acceptability which any public moral order must satisfy namely, the minimization of the infliction of harm and suffering and the just distribution of burden and benefits.

It follows from the foregoing that one major task of moral education is to assist children to develop the appropriate skills and judgment to cope with the variety of moral choices they must encounter in the technological and complex world of today. (Maqsud, 1983, in Aminigo, 2006). These principles are further discussed by Nduka (1983) who states that the aims of moral education in the Nigerian school context should be:

1. the promotion of the apprehension of, and intellectual commitment to norms.
2. the development of such skills as the ability to make sound and autonomous moral judgments.
3. the promotion of moral conduct.

Constraints To Effective Moral Education In Nigeria

In the view of Nsirim (2006) educating the citizenry on the moral demands of the society has been a tasking job for all and sundry. Many reasons have been adduced for the possible problems militating against effective moral education in the Nigerian society. Nduka and Iheoma (1983) identified the major constraints to effective moral education among others as:

1.   Lack of proper parental care which is caused largely by the socio-economic status of the family. Ignorance of the parents in useful child rearing habits; absence of strong religious background of the family; poor interpersonal relationships in the family, and love-starved family life.
2.   Over-dependence of the family on the schools as the sole agent for imparting moral education.
3.   The inability of the school system to meet up with the task because of large class size, low quality and quantity of teachers, untrained school administrators, effect of societal values on the curriculum, and the craze for paper qualification.
4.   Undisciplined homes which pollute the school environment and cause undue parental interference in the administration of schools.
5.   Conflict between school values and family values.
6.   Diminishing role of the community, the church, and other socializing agencies.
7.   Heterogeneity of the communities.
8.   Inadequate resources (human and material), for moral education (p. 21).

The Need For Moral Education In Nigerian Schools

There is an urgent need for moral education to occupy a prominent position in the Nigerian school curriculum. This is because there are various strategies that have been employed both within and outside the school system for the moral upbringing of Nigerian citizens without positive results. These include disciplinary methods, religious instruction, civic education, and the different ethical revolutions that have been instituted by various Nigerian Heads of State. Indeed, moral education is one of the basic tools for ensuring good moral behavior. Also, the school as a seat of education has a vital role to play in moral education.

Kneller (1976) is of the view that education is a moral enterprise. He stressed that teachers are always drawing attention of what ought to be said and done and how students ought to behave. Barrow (1979) believes that moral education is relevant to everybody who makes moral judgments about others either by praising or condemning other people's actions. But he also stressed that it is of relevance to teachers especially in issues such as what form of punishment may be justifiably employed and under what circumstance in schools.

In addition, moral education is relevant in ensuring a smooth and harmonious running of schools and other educational centres. These schools and educational centres would hardly be able to accomplish their primary tasks if stealing, quarreling, intolerance, and lack of respect for other persons were to flourish within them. Since the school is one of the basic agents of socialization, it is the appropriate place for the moral development of young people through education.

Morality In Nigerian Schools In The Past (1950S-1980S)

In the past, and more specifically in the 1950s to the 1980s, Nigerian schools were properly and adequately organized. There were efficient and dedicated teachers and non-teaching staff from the primary to the tertiary level of education. This was why they were highly respected in the society.

Schools at that time had facilities such as teaching materials, spacious accommodation, well equipped libraries, and science laboratories for effective teaching and learning. The reading culture among students was also encouraged. Students and pupils were socialized by way of career choice and good habits. There was nothing like examination malpractice at that time. In this way students /pupils were able to be confident enough to defend their certificates at home and abroad.

Periodically inspectors were sent to inspect the various schools. They also monitor the activities of these schools for their effectiveness. This routine exercise enables teachers to be more serious with their work.

During this period most of the students were in Boarding schools. In the boarding schools hostel masters and mistresses with the assistance of prefects, worked tirelessly to control and regulate the conduct and movement of students who were kept under strict control and were not allowed to move out of the hostels without permission. Students were punished whenever they violated the rules of the school either by suspension or even summary expulsion depending on the gravity of the offence. The resultant effect of this was that students were highly disciplined, morally sound and had respect for their teachers, other elders in society, and constituted authorities.

In the boarding houses table manners were introduced aside from attention to acceptable modes of dressing. They were also taught the need to keep their uniforms and other clothing and their entire environment clean. The students and pupils were given all round education which implied that they were adequately nurtured and moulded in character and in learning. All of these together prepared young people for participation in the society as disciplined persons.

Morality In Nigerian Schools Today

Probably because moral education is not in the curriculum of Nigerian schools we see students currently exhibiting unhealthy behaviours such as stealing, gambling, smoking, prostitution, examination malpractice, cultism, and so on. Barrow (1979) is of the view that where there are no moral lessons, that is, teachers watching over the moral development of their pupils and students, unhealthy attitudes develop, more so the children come from different backgrounds and exposures. In such a situation they will be confused on the proper moral attitudes to follow because schools are operating without a defined standard of behaviour.

It is therefore an imperative for children to be adequately directed, controlled, and guided morally in schools at all levels of the education system. This is of vital importance since they will have to take up moral questions and moral decisions later in life (Bebebiafiai, 2000).

It is however pertinent to state that those in charge of the moral education of young people have to be morally upright themselves. Wilson (1976) opines that teachers who are not punctual to school or are absent cannot expect regular and punctual attendance from their pupils. To him, the conduct of teachers in schools is more important in establishing standards, it will tend to be copied by the children.

Barrow (1979) believes that the business of moral education is not to allow the blind to lead the blind. Indeed, what we expect our teachers to do is for them to understand the problem involved in attempting to establish moral judgments since our children and youths will pass on this understanding to others in the future.

There are other factors that contribute to our teachers' inability to control pupils and students in schools. This includes population explosion in schools, deemphasizing corporal punishment, mass promotion of students in schools especially at the Junior Secondary School (JSS) level and the fact that the boarding school system in Nigerian schools has been scrapped. Other areas are lack of suitable accommodation facilities and learning materials to enhance teaching and learning in classroom settings. For Nigerians to achieve the purpose of grooming our children and youths morally and otherwise we must provide a child-friendly school environment. Thus, Akinbote (2010) states that:

> The school in modern societies provides the intellectual, social, and moral experiences from which children develop the skills, knowledge, interest, and abilities that characterize them as individuals and shape their abilities to perform adult roles (p. 22).

It has become an imperative to include moral education in the Nigerian education system through a well-designed curriculum. Plato's injunction remains real today: what the society want in the state must put in the school. If we want a morally upright citizenry, it is in the schools that the foundation should be installed.

The Place Of Moral Education In The Nigerian Education System

Moral education should be seen as an integral part of the education enterprise; without it education is not complete. Hammed (1997) believes that moral education involves stimulating the development of knowledge and channeling the use of such knowledge for the welfare of society. The task of knowledge development must be geared towards the development of positive attitudes and outlook and a willingness to reflect these in our behaviours. The commencement of this development should be at the primary, secondary, and tertiary levels of education. This is obvious when linked with the studies of Piaget (1932) and Kohlberg (1958, 1970, 1976) which have shown that moral development progresses in an invariant manner from relatively primitive low levels to more mature higher levels of functioning. More importantly they emphasize the importance of an appropriate enabling environment for the effective transition from lower to higher levels of morality. This means that our schools should be conducive enough for this transition.

In the opinion of Anyacho (2001) the content of moral

education should be selected from the major political, socio-logical, cultural, economic, environmental, and religious issues in the country. Kay (1975) in Anyacho (2001) stresses that the ethical and moral dimensions must always be borne in mind while considering the curriculum for moral education. Curriculum designers should select broad but crucial areas of learning experiences through which admirable moral values could be inculcated in Nigerian students. Moral education can be achieved through the following:

1. Religious lessons
2. Literature lessons
3. The study of history
4. Music/Arts lessons
5. Social studies/civic education
6. Individual teachers and their subjects
7. Games and sports
8. Position of responsibilities
9. Other social activities (Ogbonda, 2006).

In personal life, good moral background is the source of success and social growth and progress. It is in schools that the foundation can be laid and possibly perfected.

Moral education can enhance the development of reasoning ability (Bebebiafiai, 2008). Training students to reason also means training them to be critical. It encourages them to ask questions, seek evidence, scrutinize alternatives, and be critical of their own ideas as well as those of others. It is their evaluation of what they see or hear that will determine what ideas they will accept eventually.

The teaching of subjects related to moral education should be done in a morally and pedagogically acceptable manner. In the teaching and the development of morality in learners, dialogue as a method of teaching is emphasized. Dialogue is any form of communication between persons and groups in a spirit of sincerity and trust to achieve truth and good human relationship. Oroka (2010) holds that since dialogue involves critical reflection and thinking, reality is in constant transformation and in constant process, which is like Socratic dialectics. There are other models of teaching moral education in the view of Okoh (1998). These include:

10. Rational building model
(ii) The values classification model
(iii) The Cognitive-Development model
11. The consideration model
12. The social action model among others.

The teachers of today have a far-reaching role to play so as to mould aright the attitudes and ideals of the new generation in order to develop the Nigerian children. But the starting point is the moral level of the teacher; the corrupt school teacher is the greatest enemy of society for a teacher's role is eternal. It is for this reason that Ukeje (1986) states, "as the teacher, so is the taught."

Suggestions

The dream of a morally sound Nigeria can become reality if the following are done:

1. Inclusion of moral education in the Nigerian educa-tion system.
(ii)   Only qualified teachers should be recruited to teach the relevant subject areas in moral education in schools. This is so because the condition under which education can be made to serve the expressed aspirations of the country re-volves round the quality of the teacher.
(iii)   Other agencies – the community, the home, government, and religious groups should complement the efforts of the school.
2. Religious studies should be given prominence in the school system with modifications in syllabuses to re-flect moral principles accepted within a cultural mi-lieu.
3. Encouragement of co-curricular activities such as games, clubs, and guidance and counselling.

4.   Teachers should be appreciated and encouraged. By this is meant that the welfare of teachers should be improved and their fringe benefits and salaries paid promptly. In this way they will be motivated to carry out their statutory duties efficiently for fruitful results.

Conclusion

Morally speaking, Nigeria as a nation is in a state of crisis. For this reason, this paper suggests the inclusion of moral education in the Nigerian education system. In this way citizens would become more morally aware. It is only when citizens of a nation are adequately educated in character and in learning that they will be able to effectively perform well on their jobs, in politics, and in all other areas of human endeavour. This will in turn develop the nation economically, politically, socially and so on.

References

Adewole, A. (1989). *Ethics and the educational community.* Jos: Fab Educational Books.

Akinbote, O. C. (2010). Creating a learner-friendly school environment in Nigeria: A veritable means of sustainable growth and development. *African Journal of Historical Sciences and Education.* 6 (1).

Aminigo, I. M. (2006), *An advanced introduction to philosophy of education.* Port-Harcourt: Zelta Research consult.

Anyacho, E. O. (2001). Curriculum imperative for quality universal basic education: A case study for moral education. In A. M. Wokocha (Ed.). *Quality education and Universal Basic Education programme - A Book of Readings.* Port Harcourt: Osia International Publishers Ltd.

Bebebiafiai, I. A. (2000). Socialization of the Nigeria child. In Q. I. Qbinaju (Ed.). *The Nigerian child: His education in a socio-*

logical and psychological environment. Surulere, Lagos: lvy Press Ltd.

Bebebiafiai, I. A. (2002). The place of moral education in Nigeria's universal basic education programme. In E. Owan (Ed.). *Teacher education and universal basic education (UBE) - Annual book of readings.* Philosophy of Education Association of Nigeria.

Bebebiafiai, I. A. (2008). *Introduction to philosophy of education and some contemporary issues in the Nigerian education system.* Owerri: Cape Publishers Int'l Limited.

Bebebiafiai, I. A. (2010). *Education for political awareness in Nigeria and its impact on national development.* Unpublished PhD Thesis, Department of Educational Foundations, Faculty of Education, University of Port Harcourt.

Federal Republic of Nigeria (2004). *National policy on education.* Lagos: Federal Government Press.

Hammed, A. (1997). Education and moral development. In O. J. Nwanyanwu (Ed.). *Education for socio-economic and political development in Nigeria.* Abeokuta: Visual Resources.

Igbokwe, C. N. (2000). Developing patriotism through citizenship education. In A. Adewole and R. O. Bamisaiye (Eds.). *Philosophizing about African education: Challenges for a new millennium.*

Kneller G. E. (1976) *Introduction to philosophy of education.* New York: John Willey and Sons.

Maduka, C. (1994). Philosophy of general concerns of education. Benin: Society of Social Philosophy.

Gbamanja, S. P. T. (1997). *Curriculum development and implementation: New strategies for the years 2000 plus.* Port Harcourt: Paragraphics L.t.d.

Nsiadam, L. (2015). Discipline in Nigerian education: A philosophical perspective. In I. M. Aminigo and S. D. Osaat (Eds.). *Essays in Honour of Professor Joseph Donatus Okoh.* Port Harcourt:

Nsirim, K. E. (2006). Becoming a moral being: The challenges of our society. In G. E. Elechi and L. Ogbonda (Ed.). *Moral and religious education for colleges and universities.* Port Harcourt: Tower Gate Publications Company.

Ogbonda, L. (2006). The school system curriculum development and moral values in Nigeria. In G. E. Elechi and L. Ogbonda (Ed.). ibid.

Okoh, J. D. (1998). Philosophy of education (The basics). Owerri: Corporate Impressions.

Okujagu, A. A. (2006). The nature and concept of morality. In G. E. Elechi and L. Ogbonda (Ed.). op. cit.

Opajobi, E. B. (1997). Education as a panacea for national integration in Nigeria: A historical approach. In O. J. Nwanyanwu (Ed.). op. cit.

Orona, O. (2010). Relevance of philosophy of education. *Nigerian Journal of Educational Philosophy.* 1 (1).

Uchenna, N. G. (2006). Religious perspective in moral development. In G. E. Elechi and L. Ogbonda (Ed.). op. cit.

Ukeje, B. O. (1986). Issues and concerns in educational administration. Ibadan: Macmillan Nigerian Publishers.

Uriah, O. A. (2006). *Education, the school system and morality.* In G. E. Elechi and L. Ogbonda (Ed.). op. cit.

Wilson, E. (1975). *Education in practice.* Ibadan: Evans Brothers Nigerian Publishers Ltd.

PROF J. D OKOH

CHAPTER 15

PHILOSOPHY OF TECHNICAL CUM TECHNOLOGICAL EDUCATION AS A TOOL FOR NATIONAL DEVELOPMENT

James TOMBARI
Federal College of Education (Technical) Omoku, Rivers State

Abstract

The philosophy of technical cum technological education from the views of Nigeria's National Policy on Education, international scholars, and UNESCO was reviewed. Several ways by which this philosophy impacts Nigeria's development was identified. Contemporary challenges to the implementation of this philosophy in Nigeria was outlined and explained. Finally, this paper suggested ways forward.

Introduction

Technical cum Technological Education encompasses two broad types of education: technical and vocational education, and technological education. Technical education generally goes in hand with vocational education. This discipline of education involves all forms of general knowledge, the study of technologies and related sciences and the acquisition of practical skills, attitudes and understanding relating to occupations in the various sectors of economic and social life (Federal Government of Nigeria, 2004).

Technological Education refers to aspects of an educational system involving instruction in mathematics, science, technological concepts, directed towards the understanding of and ability to apply technology (Wilson, 1993). Technology education gives experiences in broad-based technology areas. Israel had already in the early 1990s began designing a technological system of education to fight the economic wars of the next century (Wilson, 1993).

Education is generally considered as the key tool for national development. Ellah (2013) defines this education as a change in behaviour towards a more positive direction. Pritchett (1996) in Alam (2007) analyzed that many countries despite having large educated population are unable to make significant progress, and that, third world development is sluggish. What then could have hindered a country's development despite having such large population of educated citizens? Perhaps the type and quality of education offered is a determinant factor.

High productivity gives a nation advantage of economies of scale and lowers the costs of production and prices of goods and services (Dike, 2013). The leading factors of production in today's global economy are: knowledge, technology, creativity and innovation (Dike, 2013). And technical and technological education has the potential to deliver these factors.

Philosophy Of Education For National Development

National development conceived as a purely economic affair is inadequate. It should be an overall social process which depends on outcome of man's endeavour to manipulate his natural environment (Abiogu, 2014). The relevance of philosophy of education to national development stems from the fact that philosophy maps out the line of thought for the methods chosen to approach life's problems. Abiogu (2014) notes that philosophy gives understanding of different ways of viewing things with respect to human existence. Hence, this paper expounds on the philosophy of technical cum technological education for national development.

Philosophy of Technical cum Technological Education

Conceptually, technical education and vocational education are regarded as parts of a whole. Thus, the National Policy on Education (FRN, 2004) considers technical education as the educational process that provides general education, the study of technologies and related sciences, and the acquisition of practical skills, attitudes, understanding, and knowledge relating to occupations in various sectors of economic and social life. In other words, technical education is associated with entrepreneurship. The National Policy on Education outlines the goals of technical education to include:

1.   Provide trained manpower in the applied sciences, technology, and business particularly at craft, advanced craft, and technical levels

2.   Provide the technical knowledge and vocational skills necessary for agricultural, commercial, and economic development.

3.   Give training and impart the necessary skills to individuals who shall be self-reliant economically.

It is noteworthy that technical education is a global practice embraced by various countries to stimulate their economy and deliver a competitive advantage. From the opinion of Prosser (1994) in Odu (2012) it can be deduced that technical education has the following philosophies:

1.   For effectiveness, the education should be fashioned in same way, same operations, using same tools and machines in respect of the occupation being prepared for.

2.   For effectiveness, the individual should be trained dir-

ectly and specifically in the thinking and manipulative habits required in the desired occupation.

3. The environment in which the trainee is prepared should resemble the environment he must eventually get employed in.

4. Every occupation has a minimum level of preparation needed to enable the trainees to obtain and retain employment in that occupation. Otherwise, the occupation will neither benefit the trainee nor the society.

To gain maximum benefits for technical and vocational education (TVE), the World Bank paper on Technical and Vocational Education (1991) recommended the following:

1. Well timed modern courses linked to local and global demand.

2. Relevant and up-to-date TVE courses to be developed.

3. Proper justification in respect of each country, that is, at which level is best to offer TVE courses.

4. Wider range of TVE courses need to be developed in terms of demand and cost effectiveness (not only for offering various courses, but also for duration, for student classification in terms of their merit, ages, job market, and so on).

On the other hand, technological education incorporates post-secondary education in technology offered in Polytechnics, Monotechnic, and College of Education Technical (FRN, 2004). The National Policy on Education (Federal Government of Nigeria, 2004) stipulates that technological education in all institutions shall strive towards the goals of tertiary education.

From the review above, the paradigm of technical cum technological education can be seen and appreciated. Developed countries value and compete based on their technical and technological competence. From the National Policy on Education, it can be observed that technical education entailed the post-junior secondary level, whereas technology education is offered in tertiary institutions. According to the National Policy on Education, technical education is provided by Technical Colleges.

The teacher-students' ratio should be 1:20. On completion, the trainees can pursue further education in advance craft/technical programme and in tertiary institutions such as Technical Colleges, Polytechnics or Colleges of Education (Technical) and Universities. The length of course in technical college, like other senior secondary school, is three years for the craft level and one year for the advanced craft level modular Trade Certificate. How then does this education impact on national development?

Impact of Technical cum Technological Education on National Development

1. Provides the society with skilled workforce for global competitiveness and economic growth. Increases the earning capacity of individuals and the standard of living Help unemployed young people and older workers get jobs. Reduce the burden on higher education. Reduce the inequality of earning between the rich and the poor.

2. **Promotes entrepreneurship education**. The ideals of technical cum technological education creates a need for entrepreneurial mindset and competence thus springing up another educational discipline – Entrepreneurship Education – which must work together simultaneously and harmoniously for a meaningful and economically satisfying national development. There is scarcely any technical or technological establishment without a marketing unit.

3. **Contributes to the culture, social life, and political decision**. Ghana's Kente is now worn not only in Ghana or by Africans alone. Nigeria's *garri* is now being exported to the western world – technical cum technological know-how, as well as innovation aid the processing and packaging of these products to meet international standards. With respect to social life, parents are eager to enroll their children in summer camps at the CCHUB (Co-Creation Hub): "a social in-

novation centre dedicated to accelerating the application of social capital and technology for economic prosperity." (DJEMBE Communications, 2016). Andela Fellowship has gained reputation in Nigeria for web, mobile, and software technology development. Thus, our national culture and values are promoted through our products. According to Lawal (2013), the Aso-oke work in Okene and South-west Nigeria has gained national and international acknowledgement. These are skills promoted by technical education, and it becomes a means to communicate our national culture and values. The prevalence of such local products gaining international attention, creates an enabling platform for bilateral relations.

4. **Contribute scientific knowledge of universal value**. Gutta-percha for example, which was used in Europe to coat the wires of submarine cables was a contribution from the South-East Asian culture (Modern Marvels, 1993; Wikipedia, 2017). Prior to the discovery of crude oil, Nigeria's palm oil served as lubricants and engine oil: this requires technical and technological know-how to harness.

5. Owing to the multidisciplinary nature of technical cum technological education, its trainees can integrate easily in the workforce.

6. Promotes citizens' participation in decision making about scientific problems and development (UNESCO, World conference, 1999). Technical cum technological education develops the citizen's critical awareness (Gil-Perez and Vilches, 2005).

7. Transmit the excitement of the stimulating challenges faced by the scientific community, both historically and in the contemporary world (Gil-Perez and Vilches, 2005). Through the study of technologies, and history of technology: biographies of inventors/innovators are revealed which spark the imagination

and creativity of younger generation towards pursuing greater heights and targets. Also, there is joy in participating in the solution to a challenging problem; it brings satisfaction knowing that one has contributed or is contributing to the future orientation.

8. **Cohesive literacy and Health**. Technical cum technological education is multidisciplinary. It combines everything from language to mathematics, and to science and applied science. Thus, the trainees not only acquire letter and number literacy, or business knowledge but, also understand the science behind the choices that was made: the choice of location, the choice of material, as well as the environmental consequences.

9. **Reduction in the rate of unemployment**. Graduates who could not secure gainful employment or do not wish to seek employment can exploit the acquired occupational skills to become self-employed and function in the 21st century. In this 21st century, there are new frontiers waiting to be conquered rather than vacant positions waiting to be occupied. Technical and vocational education provide these occupational skills. Skills obtained via technical education makes the individual an asset to himself and the nation, and less of a liability to the society. The trainee is equipped to think and create tangible products and services that solves life's daily needs, or business needs.

10. **Poverty reduction**. Technical education offers training and capacity building for both men and women which is key to poverty reduction (The Tide News online, 2012). These technical skills, knowledge, and entrepreneurial skills enable them to strive towards effective utilization of natural resources at their disposal.

11. **Rural Development**. Farm related skills and knowledge, as well as small and medium enterprises are dir-

ectly related to rural needs and demands. These skills find a ready market in the rural areas, and thus create a continuous circle of economic activity that seeks to address the yearning and needs of the rural populace. Being occupied by this economic activity, rural-urban migration is also reduced.

12. **Mitigate distance and language barriers**. Facebook's Mark Zuckerberg in his visit to Nigeria this year, noted that technology is changing business, education, and economic landscape by creating opportunities for the youth (DJEMBE Communications, 2016).

Challenges Of Implementing Technical Cum Technological Education

1. **Keeping up with technological trends in educational institutions**. This requires funds, skilled manpower, and political will to drive and implement. Many classrooms and laboratories are equipped with technologies that already outdated. Keeping up with new trend is expensive and requires continuous knowledge update and skills acquisition.

2. **Availability of technical cum technology teachers**. This field of education requires multidisciplinary skills and knowledge set which many self-acclaimed teachers neglect to acquire, thus standing as an obstacle in pursuing the ideals of technical cum technological education

3. **Political will**. In Nigeria, there is an obvious trend that the funding of almost any project or idea is largely dependent on the political will. When the political will of the ruling class does not support the ideals of technical cum technological education, this global competitive endeavour becomes neglected with respect to being monitored and supervised to achieve its goals,

but it is used to solicit and acquire funds.

4. **Class spacing, student-teacher ratio**. This is factor is commonly overlooked by both public and private institutions. In such situations, the number of students far out-weighs what a single instructor can effectively assess. But they endure this problem under the belief that it brings the desired funds and remuneration per teacher. However, not adhering to the ideals of class spacing and size for technical and technological education weakens the quality of training received by the students.

5. **Cultural resistance to change**. Technical cum technological education proposes self-reliant individuals and hence requires a little shift in societal expectations on the outcome of education. It creates a little friction with our typical African family setting – where children remain bound in financial commitment and otherwise to their parents and relatives so long as they are alive. Further worsened by the earlier type of education which was predominant in the country – 'complete your education to occupy a vacant job position'. In today's 21st century, there are new frontiers waiting to be conquered rather than an organized, laid out role and position to be occupied.

6. **Little or no knowledge of the goals and philosophy of technical cum technological education by the students**. When the philosophy behind a concept and its goals are not known, such a concept would inevitably fade and fizzle out of the mind of students. Better still they will initiate their own philosophy and goals, which is most likely to be cause friction with the founding principles. But when these philosophy and goals are known to the students, they are in a better position to plan, think and create in line with the national objective (the big picture).

Recommendations

Based on the challenges identified in this paper, the following recommendations are put forward for implementation:

1. Class spacing and teacher-students' ratio should be adhered to, so as to sustain and improve the quality of technical cum technological education

2. Sensitization, enlightenment and proper orientation on the strategies and direction of technical cum technological education should be promoted. This should seek to guide and enhance the understanding of school administrators, teachers and students alike

3. The generational mistake of reserving the philosophy and national goals of a given type of education as information meant for the management and administrators only needs to be dropped. If trainees are not purposively informed or aware of the overall philosophy and goals of the educational endeavour that they undertake, then, they will inevitably formulate theirs. Worse, they could pass through the system holding unto the false notion that they ought to be automatically gainfully employed upon completing the programme.

4. The world has become a global village. Technical cum technological education is inevitable for any nation. Hence, political will should be mustered towards expanding and advancing the potentials of technical cum technological education from every region in the country. Funds, and legal provisions for this education should be executed accordingly.

5. Technical cum technological teachers should strive for up to date skills and knowledge acquisition.

6. Development and growth are national challenges. Every citizen should appreciate where we are as a nation and maximize the opportunities and potentials

available at their disposal; make a responsible use of the resources and information available and acquire appropriate technical and technological skills.

Conclusion

The philosophy of technical cum technological education is a catalyst and worthy anchor on which to continue building Nigeria's socio-economic and cultural development: it develops citizens' awareness, imparts in the trainees a self-reliant approach to work, provides multidisciplinary skills and knowledge necessary for economic productivity. And most importantly, this philosophy is currently shaping the world: there is a competitive global market awaiting all who are technically and technologically competent and creative. To sustain the progress and growth in Nigeria's development, this philosophy should be embraced by all and given the political will to deliver on its goals and ideals.

References

Alam, G. M. (2008). The role of technical and vocational education in the national development of Bangladesh. *The Asia-Pacific Journal of Cooperative Education.* 9 (1).

DJEMBE Communications. (2016). Education and the impact of technology in Nigeria. Retrieved, June 10, 2017 from http://www.DJEMBEcommunications.com/language/en/education-impact-technology-nigeria/

Dike, V.E. (2013). Technical and vocational education: Key to Nigeria's development. Retrieved, July 22, 2016 from http://www.gamji.com/article8000/news8534.htm

Federal Republic of Nigeria (2004). *National policy on education* (4th ed.). Yaba: NERDC Press.

Gil-Perez, D., & Vilches, A. (2005). The contribution of science and technological education to citizens' culture. *Canadian Journal of Science, Mathematics, and Technology Education.*

5(2). 85-96.

Hansen, R., & Froelich, M. (1994). Defining technology and technological education: A crisis or cause of celebration. *International Journal of Technology and Design Education*. 4.179-207.

Lawal, A. W. (2013). Technical and vocational education: A tool for national development in Nigeria. *Mediterranean Journal of Social Sciences*. 4 (8). doi:10.5901/mjss.2013.v4n8p85

Lewis, T. (1992). The nature of technology and the subject matter of technology education--a survey of industrial teacher educators. A paper presented at the Annual Meeting of the American Vocational Association Conference, St. Louis, Missouri, December 4, 1992. Retrieved, August 05, 2017 from https://eric.ed.gov/?id=ED354340

Modern Marvels. Transatlantic cables. (1993). Retrieved, August 10, 2017 from   https://m.youtube.com/watch?v=RD3rlr3LlqU

Odu. K.O. (2012). Philosophical and sociological overview of vocational technical education in Nigeria. Retrieved, July 19, 2017 from
  http://www.freepatentsonline.com/article/College-Student-Journal/297

The Tide News Online. (2012). Technical education and national development. Retrieved, June 10, 2017 from   http://www.thetidenewsonline.com/2012/08/31/technical-education-an

UNESCO, World Conference on Science. (1999). Declaration on science and the use of scientific knowledge. Retrieved, April 6, 2017 from http://www.unesco.org/science/wcs/eng/key_documents.htm.

Wilson, D. N. Reforming technical and technological education. *The Vocational Aspect of Education*. 45 (3). 265-284. doi: 10.1080/0305787930450307

World Bank. (1991). *Vocational and technical education and training*. Washington, DC: The World Bank. tbari8@yahoo.com